Life is an Escape Room

How to Apply Lessons Learned
from Successful Escapeletes
to Achieving More in Life

Happy Escaping!

CHRISTINA M. EANES

JEFFREY W. EANES

Table of Contents

Introduction

Take a chance. It's the best way to test yourself. Have fun and push boundaries.

—Richard Branson

In 2016 we unknowingly began an exciting journey. For her 21st birthday, our daughter wanted to visit Harry Potter World at Universal Studios in Orlando. During some downtime, she came across a nearby escape room and implored us to do one. Our initial reaction was, "Why would anyone pay to 'lock' themselves in a room to solve puzzles?" Nevertheless, it was a birthday wish of our daughter, and trying out new things is fun, so we went for it. This experience has led to an obsession and realization that not only are these "games" fun, but they also can teach us a lot about life. They create a situation that allows for an individual to safely develop themselves if one is intentional and deliberate about their learning during the process.

What is an Escape Room?

What do you get when you combine a booby-trapped Egyptian tomb, following a pirate's treasure map, and a Sherlock Holmes mystery with an obstacle course, a hedge maze, and a playground? An escape room!

At their essence, escape rooms are games. Wikipedia defines a game as "a structured form of play, usually undertaken for enjoyment and sometimes used as an educational tool" and an escape room as "a live-action team-based game where players cooperatively discover clues, solve puzzles, and accomplish tasks in one or more rooms to progress and accomplish a specific goal in a limited amount of time."

Escape rooms have three factors in common: they are a series of challenges, grouped around a theme, and must be completed within a time limit. Escape rooms can be traditional (a location with physical engagement), virtual (virtual reality or played on an app), or boxed (an at-home variation that is similar to a board game or party game). While all types are fun, we've found that the most engaging form is traditional.

Traditional escape rooms also have what is commonly referred to as a game master. A game master is a person who assists with gameplay (either remotely or in-person) and can provide clues, nudges, additional information, or clarification. Based on the structure of the room, a game master can play a significant role in the flow and immersion of the game. In competitive games, they judge whether penalties will be assessed, limits on clues, and successful completion of all objectives. In non-competitive games, they help monitor your time, point out overlooked items, and can provide entertainment and banter while you play.

Many escape rooms have traditional themes (tomb, murder mystery, pandemic, and so on). But as more rooms are popping up, we're seeing rooms exploring movie and game themes, sensory themes (e.g., all dark, or no sound), and improved technology and interaction (hybrid/combined traditional and virtual reality).

Escape rooms are becoming a worldwide phenomenon. Mike van Hoenselaar, of Escape Rooms Netherland, estimated that there are approximately 8,253 locations worldwide, containing around 20,274 rooms, with a growth of 171% in 3 years in a $2 billion market! His estimates for escape rooms in the United States closely aligns with Lisa Spira, of Room Escape Artist, who is tracking about 2,350 U.S. locations. Room Escape Artist has seen a leveling off of rooms since 2018, after a dramatic increase since 2015 (about a 2,300% increase from only 100 U.S. locations in 2015).

We collected some data ourselves on the escape room market. Exploring U.S. Census Bureau data using the North American Industry Classification System (NAICS) codes showed that the Arts, Entertainment, and Recreation market in the U.S. has grown over 48% between 2009 and 2018. When you consider that the population between 26 and 54 years old has increased less than 1% over the same period, and inflation over the same period only accounts for about 16.6%, then the entertainment market in the U.S. has been particularly strong. Coupling this data with a dramatic increase in the number of escape rooms suggests that they are here to stay.

What is an Escapelete?

An athlete is a person trained in a sport or other form of physical exercise, leading to exceptional skills in their chosen sport. An escapelete is an escape room athlete – an individual who is proficient in making it through an escape room experience while honing their skills as an individual and as a team member.

Like good athletes, good escapeletes benefit from the work done to better themselves in all aspects of their life: generating self-confidence, physical and mental agility, self-improvement, and continuous learning.

Why is Life an Escape Room?

Once the escape room addiction commenced, we quickly discovered that the skills necessary to work through an escape room experience translated well into being successful in life. We recognized that escape rooms are an excellent metaphor for life, and the skills that help you successfully escape are the same ones you need to achieve what you desire in life: better relationships, more financial freedom, happiness, and so on.

Sure, escape rooms are used in the corporate team building arena, but we found that the same skills can be applied to life in general, making us better human beings. We decided to become proficient escapletes and share our learning experiences.

How to Read this Book

This book is composed of lessons and observations. Some of the lessons build off of each other; however, for the most part, you can skip through and read the ones that you may need to "hear" at the moment. Each chapter contains a *Reflections* section to deepen your self-awareness for each lesson.

In each lesson, we share one to several examples of learning from our escape room adventures; however, we purposely do not share enough information to identify the specific escape room or company involved. We do not want to ruin the experience for others. To view our current recommended escape room companies by location (that we have personally experienced), visit Escapeletes.com.

Pro Tips

After completing as many escape rooms as we have, we are often asked whether they start to get repetitive or easy. The answer is no (kudos to all the ingenuity out there). While we want everyone to use the lessons to help improve all aspects of their lives (including escaping rooms), for fun, we have included hints that have helped us improve our escape room experiences. Happy Escaping!

Lesson #1: What You Need Is Often In Plain Sight

After taking a while to escape our cells, we crept into the cell block hallway. We deciphered a code on the walls, which activated a secret passageway that led into what appeared to be a utility/drainage basement. Once the smoke cleared, we had to move the body of a guard, solve a couple of other puzzles, and then activate another secret passage to the Warden's office

Once in the office, we were dismayed to find that there were less than 10 minutes left to thoroughly search the office and locate the code to turn off the alarm, which would soon alert the local authorities to our break out attempt. With the lights flashing, the clock ticking down, and the anxious feeling of the impending arrival of the police, we got stuck – we couldn't uncover the code.

Fortunately, we had gone through many escape room experiences at this point, using the fun to develop ourselves intentionally and realized that the atmosphere of an escape room, along with the pressure of time, could narrow our perception. The psychological term for this is *inattentional blindness*, which means that even on our best days, we tend not to notice things that are right in front of us. The span of things that we can "see" and comprehend is constricted to a very narrow point. Throw in a bit of overload with either panic or new stimuli, and it gets even worse. With this knowledge, learned through both these created experiences and situations that have occurred in real life, we took a step back, took a few deep breaths, and initiated another look around the office with "new" eyes. There it was! The code was right in front of us all along! The books on the bookshelf were arranged in such a way that they appeared to look like a code. With just two minutes left on the countdown clock, we punched in the code and made our escape before the authorities could arrive and thwart our bid for freedom.

Too often in life, we allow for inattentional blindness to get in our way. From the supervisor's late Friday afternoon task that suddenly becomes urgent, to choosing paint colors when we're feeling tired, we can't see an opportunity or the solution that is right in front of us. We are either in a negative frame of mind or so focused on what we expect to happen, that we're not open to what else could happen. As we experience a heightening of emotion, specifically those of the "negative" variety, our ability to be aware of our surroundings or accept alternatives, dramatically decreases. To overcome this form of blindness, you must become aware of when it is occurring and develop ways in which you can reduce its effect on you. Effective solutions vary based on the individual; however, any way you can reach a state of calm usually works, such as deep breathing, meditation, physical exercise, or some other healthy means to calm the mind.

Reflections

1. How and when are you allowing inattentional blindness to get in your way?
2. What are some ways you can identify when you have heightened your inattentional blindness?
3. Once you've identified that you are currently experiencing a heightened inattentional blindness, what are some ways you can increase your openness to perceiving more?

Lesson #2: Step Back And Look At The Big Picture

We found ourselves in yet another cell block; however, this one was more dungeon-like and in another country. It is incredible how many times we have voluntarily gone to prison – maybe it is the excitement of the handcuffs and bars? Unfortunately, we were not able to break out of this one before the guard returned from her lunch break, which turned into a big lesson for us.

Here's what happened – there was a map of the cell block on the wall with emergency exits (very useful for prison breaks). A close examination of the map appeared to indicate that there was a secret compartment in one of the rooms. Perhaps that was the location of the tools we needed to secure our release? We carefully searched and searched in the area indicated on the map and came up with nothing. Two minutes to go until the guard came back, and we could feel the building emotion and fear related to not escaping in time. Suddenly, we were too late. Our time was up, and the guard returned! She showed us that if we had just stepped back and examined the walls of the cell block from a distance, we would have noticed huge numbers painted on them.

How did we miss the huge numbers? They looked like weird markings up close, but it wasn't until you looked at them from a distance that you could see the numbers. We were so mired in the details that we didn't step back and look at the big picture. Thankfully, since this was an escape room experience and not a real prison, we were released to enjoy the next escape room and consolatory ice cream.

Not too long after that experience, we found ourselves in a video rental store. We wondered if we got caught in a time warp since these stores mostly no longer exist (do people still watch DVDs?). There was so much nostalgia in the room that we yet again found ourselves focusing on the details and getting stuck at finding a clue. Remembering our lessons learned, one of us took a step back and viewed everything from a distance. This simple action allowed us to notice that there was a weird grouping on one of the walls – which ended up revealing a code.

Reflect on this important lesson and how it applies to life in general. Think about ways in which getting stuck in the details (also known as "the weeds") can get in our way. Often we are so focused on the little things that we neglect to step back and look at the bigger picture. This lesson can be applied to many areas of our lives. We can get so focused on the tasks related to a project that we don't step back to see if we're still going in the right direction. Are we so focused on the small, seemingly negative exchanges within a relationship, that we haven't stepped back to see if there is a way we can better communicate, or if it is even worth having this person in our life? Think about where you are currently stuck in the details in your life and how stepping back to look at the big picture would be beneficial.

Reflections

1. In what current situations do you need to look at the big picture?
2. How can you best remove yourself from the details of the situation to give you an objective, full view perspective?
3. Once you've done this, what are you now going to do differently based on your new perspective?

Lesson #3: Consider What Is Missing

We found ourselves in a basement – a very 1980's basement. Rumor has it that someone's grandmother had passed away and, before she went to the great beyond, she hid a million dollars in her basement. Being the adventurer that she was, she created a series of tests for individuals to overcome. Only those who could surpass all of the challenges would be deemed worthy enough to find and keep the money.

After thoroughly searching the basement, we had uncovered a bunch of alphabet letters from various places. Remember those alphabet letters that had magnets to create fun words and phrases on the refrigerator door? Grandma kept them and hid them throughout her basement. We were able to find 22 different letters of varying sizes and colors, but couldn't figure out how to arrange them to give us a four-letter code. We tried to form words or arrange them by size or color, but to no avail. After several tries, we realized that we were missing four-letters of the alphabet, and (duh!) there was a four-letter combination lock just waiting to be opened. After identifying the four missing letters, we were able to do a word scramble and discover the code we needed (a lot of singing our ABC's was involved).

So often in life, when we want to change something about ourselves, we are focused only on what we've gained during the process of making that change. Sometimes we need to reflect on what is no longer there to determine just how far we've come through that change. For example, let's say you've wanted to work on your relationship with someone in your life – your work colleagues, your boss, your significant other, a friend, and so on. You focus on how you can better communicate with this person and work hard on mending that relationship to get it to a better place. Soon, your conversations are going smoothly, and you forget how difficult it used to be to attempt to communicate with this person. Remembering what is missing helps you realize just how far you've come and how hard you worked. It also enables you to solidify your learning into improving future relationships.

Reflections

1. Where in your life do you need to examine what is missing to celebrate success?
2. What are some strategies for helping yourself to look at what is missing?
3. How can you train yourself to look for what is missing in the future?

Lesson #4: Approach With A Beginner's Mind

We found ourselves in Camelot, and we were excited to learn that King Arthur and the Knights of the Round Table had decided that the time had come for a new champion. They had created a series of challenges to test worthy adventurers and had Merlin seal Excalibur back in its stone. We were up for the challenge and knew that we would be the next champions.

We breezed through the first room of challenges and were feeling very knightly. As we entered the second room of quests, we found small figurines with symbols on them that we had seen several times before – we were experts in escape rooms after all. Based on the symbols, we knew we had to look for a cipher. We looked throughout the second room for the cipher, and after coming up with nothing, we searched the first room where we started our quest from top to bottom.

Finally, we asked the suit of arms in the room for help (the game master's ingenious method of communication) and received a clue that revealed we had everything we needed. So we went back to examine the figurines and their "playing" board again and figured out the solution to the puzzle.

We were able to liberate the sword and become the new champions of Camelot; however, our prior experience almost led to failure. When we get into conversations with others about our escape room adventures, we often hear the comment, "You must get out of rooms so fast now." The answer is, "No, we don't." Prior experience can be both a blessing and a curse.

When we become experts through our knowledge and experience in different areas, we must become aware of how our expertise can get in our way. We may think we have something figured out, but because we have the tunnel vision that an expert's mind can create, we often might not see the simple solutions that are in front of us. The solution for this is to design the circumstances that will allow us to adopt a beginner's mindset. Strategies could include bringing along a beginner and asking them to share their thoughts or asking yourself, "What's another way I can look at this?" and pretending that you've never encountered the problem before.

Reflections

1. In what areas of your life do you need to adopt a beginner's mind?
2. What strategies can you use for employing a beginner's mind?
3. What are some alternative solutions that you wouldn't have come up with had you not employed a beginner's mind?

Lesson #5: Creative Problem-Solving Is A Must

We found ourselves trapped in the dark backstage of a theater. After a few minutes, we found a control panel that allowed us to get some of the lights working so we could see the backstage area a little better. We quickly went about our process of searching the room for items we could use to liberate ourselves. Finding a wrench, we immediately began to look around for a nut/bolt combination to unscrew, perhaps uncovering a secret compartment containing a key to the chest in the room.

After several minutes of searching, we were unable to locate the item we assumed the wrench was supposed to open. We set it aside, thinking that once we gained access to the dressing room, it would come in handy. We were able to find the code to the dressing room and searched thoroughly but still could not find anything that we could use it on.

We came to a point where we were stuck. We couldn't figure out what to do next. As we were brainstorming what to do, one team member started playing with the wrench near one of the walls that had exposed pipes and found the wrench stuck to one of the pipes. It was magnetized! We moved the wrench along the plumbing and soon found that it attached itself to what sounded like a key inside one of the pipes. We moved the key along the pipes, and it soon dropped out of one of them.

What had held us back in this experience was something called *functional fixedness*, which is an issue that tends to get in everyone's way, especially when problem-solving. Functional fixedness is a psychological term describing how we limit ourselves to use an object only in its intended manner. This limit to our perception was uncovered in the mid-1900s through Gestalt psychologist Karl Duncker's candle problem. In this cognitive performance test, he would present an individual with matches, a small cardboard box of thumbtacks, and a candle. He tasked each person to fix and light the candle on a corkboard wall in a way so that the candle wouldn't drip wax on the table below. Participants in this assessment would try many different variations, most failing to accomplish the task. Because the thumbtacks were in the box, they didn't think of the box as having any other potential function. For example, removing the thumbtacks and using them to fix the box onto the corkboard, then putting the candle in the box.

When engaging in problem-solving concerning areas of your life, reflect on potential areas where functional fixedness is holding you back. Perhaps you believe that your electronic calendar can only be used to track meetings and appointments when you can use it to schedule in blocks of time to work on specific tasks? Or maybe you are throwing out pickle jars when you are done with them at home and then buying containers at the store in which to keep various small items?

Reflections

1. Reflect on potential areas in your life where functional fixedness is holding you back.
2. What are some ways in which you can engage in more creative problem-solving?
3. What are some strategies you can implement to ensure you overcome functional fixedness?

Lesson #6: Change Your Perspective

We've had to save the world from several potential outbreaks of the zombie virus, and this was, yet again, another mad scientist we had to thwart. We found ourselves in his kitchen and knew that he had a secret lab on the premises where he was experimenting on humans and ways to release the virus for mass exposure. We thought it was interesting that he had a chain and lock around his refrigerator, so we found a code to unlock it and found the entrance to a secret crawl space!

After crawling through the walls to another room, we found the lab. We were so close to our final mission – accessing the virus and neutralizing it. To do this, we had to find a four-digit code. We looked EVERYWHERE in the lab, including searching through a zombie corpse (yuck!). Knowing we've had to train ourselves to change our perspective, we took another look at the room. What's different? What's out of place?

The lab was very clinical – no personal effects whatsoever – except for framed art on the counter. We picked up the frame and looked at it, marveling at what a weird picture it was as it seemed to be a barcode of some sort. Thinking of ways we could change our perspective, we looked at the frame from different viewpoints: upside down, sideways, and at all angles. As we tilted the frame, all of a sudden, the lines formed four digits. We found the code! We quickly entered it into the case and neutralized the virus, saving the world yet again (you're welcome!).

Unfortunately, as we go through life, we tend to look at every person, situation, or problem from the same perspective, not training ourselves to look at the subject from different angles. We severely limit ourselves and our abilities to navigate life when we don't do this successfully. How does this limit us? By only solving problems the same way each time, by not changing how we view a person's behavior and reacting to them the same way each time, or by responding the same way when a situation presents itself over and over again; all of these are unproductive responses.

A great way to retrain yourself to look at things from a different perspective is to argue with yourself. For example, let's say you've decided that an individual you interact with regularly likes to be difficult for the sake of being difficult. Ask yourself the following questions:

1. What belief do I have about this person's intentions?
2. What are the facts? NOT the assumptions I've made about their behavior.
3. What is another way I can view their behavior?

If you have trouble getting out of your perspective, get creative by asking yourself about different viewpoints that others would have about this situation. How would [insert name] interpret this behavior? What would my cat/dog think? What would that plane flying overhead say about the situation? It sounds funny to do and may feel a bit awkward at first, but it does help you get out of your perspective.

Reflections

1. When you feel stuck in a situation, ask yourself, what is another way I can view this?
2. Who do I know that thinks differently than me, and how can I ask them for advice on overcoming a troublesome situation?
3. What weird and wacky perspectives can I take to see this situation from a different vantage point?

Lesson #7: Check Your Assumptions At The Door

If you're not familiar with escape rooms, before entering each room, the game master briefs the players on the rules of the location. The rules are very similar across locations in both the United States and other countries, generally including the following: no climbing, no moving furniture or flooring, do not use force (no breaking things!), don't touch the electrical cords, and so on.

Not long after we started our escape room adventures, we found ourselves locked in a jail cell in the captain's cabin of a pirate ship in the Dominican Republic. Being in the DR, there were no health and safety codes, so we were genuinely locked in a jail cell for 60 minutes. After the game master briefed us on the rules (which we barely listened to as we were becoming experts by this point – or so we thought), she turned out the lights and left. Feeling around in the dark, we were able to locate a flashlight to look around the cell and in the room beyond. We spotted the keys on the wall across from the jail cell! We searched some more and found a pole that was attached to one of the cell bars with a lock. All we needed to do was find the code for the lock, and we could free ourselves from the cell.

About eight minutes of searching had passed by at this point. We have developed a rule to ask for help if we spend more than five minutes stuck on a given task. We grabbed the walkie talkie to communicate with the game master, and she hinted that we should look at the rug on the floor. We moved the carpet out of the way and found the clue that would give us the code to get the pole and fish for the key across the room. We ended up escaping the room with two minutes to spare;

however, if we had not assumed that the rules are all the same from location to location, then we would have listened more closely to the game master's pre-brief and asked if we could move furniture or flooring. Lesson learned – we listen carefully, even hundreds of games later, and ask if we don't hear a rule to which we've become accustomed.

In life, we do this as well – how are the assumptions you've made about the "rules" in your professional or personal life gotten in your way? Just because something has always been done a certain way, does that mean that it always will be done a certain way?

Reflections

1. What assumptions have you made about the "rules" in your life?
2. What are some strategies you can use to test those assumptions?
3. How will you check your assumptions next time you come across a "rule?"

Lesson #8: Beware Of Red Herrings

Tomb raiding can be quite exhausting (and fun!). The memory is lost on whose tomb we were raiding, but we were minutes from getting our prize – a huge ruby. We snuck past the guardians in the ante-chamber; opened the sarcophagus, thus retrieving the code to the treasure chamber; and filled a bag full of sand to match the weight of the ruby. Now, all we had to do was make our way over some rock tiles with weird hieroglyphs to steal the ruby and exit the tomb.

We searched high and low throughout all of the chambers to determine the hieroglyphic order to step on the stone tile path. We were able to identify some of the markings, but not all were present in all of the chambers. Even with some identified, we couldn't find anything concerning the order they should be stepped on. After a while, we got frustrated and just walked across the stone tiles to replace the ruby with the bag of sand. The exit door opened!

After our exit, the game master asked if we had any questions. Of course, we immediately asked about the stone tiles. He laughed and said that he has a lot of fun watching folks trying to figure out the path and that it was a "red herring." The term "red herring" came from the 1800s when a strong-smelling fish was used to divert hounds from chasing a hare. It is now used to denote a distraction – something that can take us away from our goal. Not all escape room locations use them, but we have found ourselves distracted in ones that do.

In life, many things divert us from going after our goals. These diversions can be internal, such as our assumptions, constraining beliefs, and the level of confidence we have in achieving the goal. They can also be external, such as little everyday tasks that get in the way of focusing our time and energy on the target. Let's reflect on the red herrings you are currently experiencing in your life and how you can move them aside.

Reflections

1. What is happening internally that is diverting you from going after your goal(s)?
2. What is happening externally that is diverting you from achieving your goal(s)?
3. What strategies will you implement to make sure you stay focused on your goal (both internally and externally)?

Lesson #9: Use Occam's Razor

We had been in space for a while when things took a turn for the worse. Our ship was in lockdown, and we were hurling toward a star. And, on top of everything else, all the instructions on the control panels were in Russian! As we were resetting the order to a system readout, we found that we couldn't move the needed piece either left, right, up, or down. We needed it to move diagonally to the upper right. After spending an unnecessary amount of time on it, a fellow cosmonaut, in passing, suggested we try to move it to the upper right, and it worked. Our preconceived notion of how things might be constrained prevented us from picking the most obvious solution.

Occam's razor is the idea that the simplest solution is most often the correct one, a principle that "entities should not be multiplied without necessity." In other words, Keep It Simple, Silly (KISS). In many aspects of life, we find ourselves making things much more difficult than we should, whether it is trying to find a reason for how a problem occurred or trying to find a solution for said problem. It could be that we worry ourselves unnecessarily about an upcoming challenge we have to face, only to find that all of that worry was for naught – everything turned out fine. Or we fretted over a big project and procrastinated on beginning the various tasks, but found that it wasn't as bad once we got started.

Reflections

1. Reflect on a time when you were worried about how hard something might have been, but when it was done, it seemed easy. What could you have done differently to save yourself the grief?
2. In what ways can you think about a daunting task or action differently so that it could be easier in the future?
3. When you're stuck on a complicated problem, how might a child answer it?

Lesson #10: Execute A Search Warrant

As we've noted in previous lessons, it is important to tune out distractions as well as not to allow yourself to get diverted by red herrings. At the same time, you need to teach yourself to scan your environment to notice everything – like you're executing a search warrant.

We found ourselves in yet another cabin in the woods, but this time, instead of a serial killer, Sasquatch, zombie horde, or pack of werewolves coming after us (coincidentally they are always 60 minutes away from getting us), we were taking part in the California Gold Rush. Yep – we were there to find gold! Once we broke into the cabin, we found our way to the gold mine underneath, surprisingly through the fireplace.

Before we could blow up the mine to find the gold (and, yes, we did blow up the shaft), we had to find a bunch of wooden puzzle pieces. When arranged correctly, the puzzle would provide us with instructions for placing the dynamite and setting it off. We had to carefully scan the environment as the pieces were everywhere within the cave and even outside of the mine shaft. It took both of us examining each square inch of the surrounding areas to ensure we didn't miss any pieces and were able to liberate the gold.

Are you in the habit of scanning your environment? This applies to many levels, from your personal safety to achieving your goals. Let's start with safety. Do you continually scan your environment, looking for unusual behavior, or identifying exits in case there is an emergency? Next, we'll move toward the achievement of goals: are you continually scanning your environment for opportunities to help you achieve your goals? Opportunities to help you achieve your goals are around every corner, so it is vital to take the time to look for them. Starting up a conversation at the coffee shop or on the plane while you're traveling could lead to a new job, a fruitful connection in your professional network, or even the love of your life (if you haven't already met them).

Reflections

1. To what extent are you scanning your environment for new opportunities?
2. What are some strategies you can use to improve how you scan your environment for opportunities?
3. How can you ensure you are in the present moment to better scan your environment? (For example, put the phone down!)

Pro Tip #1: Guessing

What if I told you that only knowing three digits in a four-digit lock was good enough?
—Escape Room Meme

There are some purists out there who believe that each puzzle or challenge in an escape room should be figured out and can be logically derived from elements within a room. However, in practice, some rooms might have inadvertently, or intentionally, left some codes to be inferred or deduced. Or they may have even accidentally forgotten necessary information or expect their players to have prior outside knowledge. In many ways, figuring out puzzles and tasks are as much about managing the game designers and game masters as about the idealized "information available." Which brings us to the topic of guessing.

Fairly early in our escape room journey, we had come upon a three-digit lock, and we found three digits, but we could not find what order they should be put into the lock. When asked, the game master said, "guess." A light bulb came on (figuratively). Since one of us majored in mathematics in college, it was a little embarrassing to realize there were only six ways three digits could be put into the lock (a roughly 20-second task).

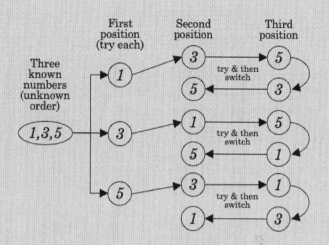

The example shows what is sometimes called "brute force" (not to be confused with that other brute force method called "breaking things" ...let's not do that kind of "technique"). The concept of *brute force* comes from cryptography and is an attempt at trying every possible combination. However, since it takes about three seconds to try a single combination, at best, it should be reserved for times when there are 10 or fewer possibilities (e.g., one digit of a four-digit code, when the rest are correct and in the correct place). Even trying the above example on a four-digit lock with known numbers and unknown order would take about two minutes, provided you did it correctly. And, attempting brute force on a three-digit lock (1000 possibilities x 3 per second = 50 minutes) is less than optimal for a 60-minute room.

Because of the quirkiness of some locks and the possibility of rushing over the correct code, we only recommend this for when you know the three digits of a three-digit lock, guessing one digit on a combination lock, or guessing the orientation of a single object (e.g., whether that pesky statue should face north, south, east, or west).

Warning: Some locations frown at guessing while others don't mind the ingenuity. Be careful; we were once docked six minutes (six minutes!) and failed to get out of a room because a player was playing with a three-switch lock, each with three positions (a total of 27 possible combinations). While we weren't trying to guess, by sheer luck, the correct code was identified, and the hatch opened. When asked if we had completed the puzzle without guessing, we were honest and said no. And the gamemaster took some of our time away. We failed to get out of the room at the last puzzle, which was probably less than a 6-minute puzzle. Bummer.

Lesson #11: Tune Out Distractions

Since we like to save the world regularly, we thought we would sign up for a mission to overthrow Krampus and save Christmas for all the little boys and girls. To do this, we found ourselves breaking into his cabin in the woods. The cabin was full of Christmas cheer, but it also felt very creepy. After we overcame a few challenges, we found a secret access area to his workshop. Unfortunately, we got stuck in this access area because there were hundreds of keys hanging from the ceiling, and we heard several little voices yell out, "pick me, pick me, pick me," and they wouldn't stop! They became so distracting that we had to take a moment to stop, breathe, and focus.

After getting a clear head, we looked up and started examining the keys. After a few minutes of close observation, we were able to see that one key was not like the others, grabbed it, and opened the door to the workshop. We ended up saving Christmas that day, but it was a close one!

You know that crazy feeling you get when there is so much competing for your attention? Life can throw a lot of things at us at once, and it is hard to weed through all the distractions to determine what is essential. So many things can seem crucial that it takes a calm and observant focus to weed out the not-so-important stuff.

There are two different methods to help us do just that: the Prioritization Matrix and the Impact/Feasibility Matrix. The first is the Prioritization Matrix, which compares the importance versus the urgency of each task. With this tool, you look at each task that is on your to-do list and decide the level of importance to get it done: from very important to not important. Then you look at the level of urgency in getting it done: from urgent to not urgent. After assessing each task, you organize them by priority: tasks that are both urgent and important, you do right away; tasks that are important, but not urgent, schedule them in your calendar; and tasks that are urgent, but not important, delegate if at all possible; finally, dump the tasks that aren't important or urgent.

	Urgent	Not Urgent
Important	**1st Priority** Do it Now	**2nd Priority** Set Schedule and Plan
Not Important	**3rd Priority** Delegate it	**Do not prioritize** Minimize or Eliminate

IMPORTANCE

URGENCY

Another strategy to rank your tasks is the Impact/Feasibility Matrix, which compares the value versus the ability to complete the task. For this tool, you will look at the impact completing each task will have on getting you to your goals: from very impactful for moving me toward my goals to less impactful. Then list the feasibility of getting each task done: from easy to do to very hard to complete. Once you've assessed each task, you'll want to prioritize those tasks that will have the most impact on getting you toward the achievement of your goals in the most feasible way.

	Hard / Demanding	Easy / Able to Complete	
Valuable	Significant, but less easy to do because of time, resources, knowledge, skills, etc. Consider	Significant, easy to do! Do it now	*Valuable*
Not Valuable	Not significant, difficult to do! Not worth it	Not hugely significant but easy to do "Quick win"	*Not Valuable*
	Hard / Demanding	Easy / Able to Complete	

IMPACT

FEASIBILITY

Reflections

1. Reflect on how you react when there are a lot of competing tasks demanding your attention.
2. What are some strategies you can use to help yourself get to that place where you can calmly and objectively decide on what needs your attention?
3. After reaching this calm and objective state, put your task list through both the Prioritization Matrix and the Impact/Feasibility Matrix to determine what demands your immediate focus, and begin working your way through the list.

Lesson #12: Break Free Of Your Thoughts

We were a team of three this time - trapped in a military bunker by aliens. Thankfully, we work together very well as a team, we know how to come together to work on issues, and we know how to divide and conquer when necessary. Moreover, when one team member got particularly cranky as we were trying to work our way into the control room to override the bunker's security system, the rest of us were understanding and supportive, as it had been a difficult escape attempt thus far.

As we got closer to the final task required to escape the bunker (with only 10 minutes before the aliens returned to check on our captivity status), we became stumped. There was a voltage sign on the cage we had just entered. When we looked through a periscope we found in the cage, we saw the same voltage sign upside down. What was up with that? Since we work so well as a team, we each took turns trying to figure out why the sign was upside down and what it signified. It took a couple of minutes – which is a long time when you have only 10 minutes left – but one team member noticed that there was a color difference in a couple of the letters on the sign. We were looking at a completely different sign! We ended up asking for a clue to help us decipher the difference between the signs from the game master and found that we needed to identify the differences to get the code to unlock the final door.

We learned several lessons on how our mind can get in the way when we were escaping the aliens that day. The main takeaway from this successful escape is that when you expect to see something, it limits your ability to see anything else. We assumed we were looking at the same sign, with the only difference being that we were looking at it upside down, so we couldn't see anything else. This is why it is essential to keep an open mind, rely on your teammates to step in, and, ultimately, to ask for help when you're stuck.

Reflections

1. In what ways has your thinking got in your way recently?
2. How were you able to change a perception that was holding you back?
3. Who do you have in your life that can help you see things differently?

Lesson #13: Got Patience?

There were four of us on this adventure. Two of us got locked in the dungeon, and the other two were tasked with liberating the trapped team. Then all four needed to work together to escape the dingy castle of monsters and mayhem.

This was a different kind of adventure, one that our captors told us that they would return in 90 minutes rather than the usual 60 minutes. Based on this extended escape time, before being sent to the creepy castle, our team discussed all the possibilities we may face. Since we had 90 minutes to liberate ourselves, we thought we would find many rooms within the castle, each containing difficult challenges to overcome.

While our team felt immersed in the experience, after the first ten minutes of our time, we quickly found out that our captors set a longer period because it involved a lot of waiting on each team's part. One team would solve a clue that would help the other team move forward in the quest, and then have to wait on the other team to overcome a challenge before they could move forward to the next puzzle. The four of us did not come together as a team until an hour had passed. Thankfully we completed our quest less than two minutes before the evil castle dwellers returned.

Being humans, we have to work together to achieve common goals. Part of working together involves practicing patience, as we often find ourselves waiting on others to complete their part on a team project. Whether it's planning a family vacation or completing a project at work involving multiple teams, we must cultivate our patience to work well with others.

How does one cultivate patience? One strategy is once you've handed over your portion of the work, look at everything you can do on your part to help the other team members complete their component (balancing this with not getting in their way.) Another strategy is to work on something else to give your other team members the time and space they need to complete their share of the work. Don't have anything else to work on? If this is the unlikely case, take some time to develop yourself – read articles or a book, take online training, listen to a podcast, and so on.

Reflections

1. How patient are you in waiting for your fellow team members to complete their portion of the work?
2. How can you be more patient? What strategies can you implement to give them the time and space they need to work?
3. How can you assist, without becoming an obstacle, in your fellow team members' progress?

Lesson #14: Cheating Spoils The Fun

It was the early 1700s, and we found ourselves on an empty pirate ship – the captain and crew away for the night. We had overheard the captain talking about a treasure of gold and jewels hidden on the ship. To our dismay, another band of treasure hunters had overheard the same discussion, and we found ourselves teamed up to beat the captain's traps. It was obvious that these upstart glory seekers had not raided many ships before. Within the first five minutes, the other band of raiders had been a whirlwind of noise and motion (very loud and excited, but not being very productive). A pair of them had finally settled into trying to guess a four-digit lock (without any clues!). While we would never fault a profiteer from trying to guess a bit (see Pro Tip #1), jumping right to the lottery of guessing a code with 10,000 options seemed a bit brazen. They later moved on to disassembling furniture to get into drawers (to the game master's consternation).

Sometimes, we find ourselves frustrated or lost, and we resort to extreme actions with the justification that we are "thinking outside the box." If we thought about it, it would become obvious that we are not helping the situation, and we are letting down our teammates. Sometimes, we have to forgo the "easy path" and buckle down to do the necessary work. As Joe Girard says, "The elevator to success is out of order. You'll have to use the stairs one step at a time."

As we work through problems and try to succeed, short cuts have their benefits, and wasting time on unnecessary work can set us back. However, over time the effort invested in getting us to our goals is part of the benefit of getting there, both in the ethical sense and the practical sense.

Reflections

1. Have you ever taken a "short cut" that you didn't feel good about? Did others accuse you of "cheating"?
2. How does working through a solution to the current problem help you when you see a similar problem in the future? Will you be more prepared the next time?
3. Does winning feel better when earned? What happens over time to the feeling you have about success when it compromises your integrity?

Lesson #15: Prepare Like An Escapelete

At this point in our "escapelete careers," we've gone on several of what we like to call "escapecations." We will identify a city (or region) that we'd like to explore and then plan out our time visiting the area by mapping out the escape room locations and scheduling several experiences each day throughout our time there.

In our planning process, we consider where we can stay to maximize our ability to walk to locations so we can stay more active during our escapecation while also taking in the sites that the city or region has to offer. In this past year, we even tried out a cruise that would take us to multiple countries that had quality escape rooms near each port.

For us to fully enjoy these escapecations, we also plan out how we can maximize our self-care during our explorations. Some individuals have equated self-care with relaxation, which is a small part under the big umbrella of self-care. However, self-care encompasses so much more: proper nutrition, hydration, exercise, adequate sleep, developing one's mind, and so on. With self-care in mind, we plan out our escapecations to ensure that we are moving as much as possible during the day, properly fueling our bodies, staying hydrated, creating rest breaks throughout the day, and getting adequate sleep at night.

We also make sure we are taking care of ourselves when we are not on escapecations to ensure that we not only more fully enjoy our lives, but also when we do visit those escape rooms that involve climbing, crawling, or some other fun physical adventure, that we can meet the demands required of us. How cool is it that we can climb through refrigerators into crawlspaces to save humanity from a zombie virus as middle-aged adults (or even into our golden years like one of our regular teammates)?

Are you preparing for your life like an escapelete? To live a quality life that will allow us to experience all the joys around us fully, we MUST take care of ourselves. Proper weight management, nutrition, hydration, exercise, adequate sleep, emotion and stress management, and challenging your mind are imperative to living your life fully.

Reflections

1. How are you preparing for life like an escapelete?
2. What areas of health mentioned in this lesson do you need to work on?
3. What are you going to do to improve yourself to get to escapelete level?

Lesson #16: Don't Flounder In Your Frustration

Inevitably, there are moments in most escape rooms where an escaplete experiences frustration. One could be in a room where the leaps of logic are beyond what any human could make, a team could have trouble communicating on a puzzle, a teammate could be overly competitive or grumpy, a game master might be uninvolved or impose unfair sanctions on the team (see *Lesson #33: Leader Creates the Weather*), one could find themselves in the room with strangers that aren't a good fit (although this is solely a U.S. issue), or many other scenarios that could bring frustration to even the most experienced escapelete.

Each frustrating moment that presents itself is an opportunity for an escapelete to practice emotional intelligence and not just survive the frustration but thrive because of it. While there are some enthusiasts here in the United States who enjoy getting booked into a room with strangers, we generally prefer the way other countries run their rooms – private bookings only.

We've been pretty lucky getting the rooms to ourselves because we've learned the best ways to book rooms (see *Pro Tip #3: Scheduling and Getting Rooms*); however, we do end up with strangers once in a while. Our worst experiences have been when we were matched up with strangers who were drunk or just plain rude.

In one particular experience, we began a room with individuals who claimed they were quite experienced in escape rooms (they had done four). Our mission was to find our way to our current time as an evil corporation had sent us back in time and left us there.

One of our "teammates" endeavored to dominate each puzzle as we worked on it, even putting his hand in one of our faces to shush us as we attempted to help with one of the puzzles. This was a perfect opportunity for us to work through our frustration in being in the room with this man. A few deep breaths, change of perspective (or more like compassion for this man as his life must really suck if he behaves this way with everyone), and refocusing on the task at hand helped us move through the frustration and complete the mission. We made it back to our current year and were able to chalk that experience as a learning opportunity. We not only learned how to handle frustration, but we also made sure we schedule better. After all, we don't want to get "locked" in a room with an a$$hole again.

Reflections

1. How are you approaching frustrating situations in your life?
2. What are some ways you can turn these types of situations into learning opportunities?
3. What process can you implement to handle frustrating situations in the moment?

Lesson #17: Find Light In The Darkness

We had the novel adventure of doing an escape room in complete darkness while in Europe. After doing the number of escape rooms we've done, the unusual gets more and more exciting (and a bit scary as well!). Going into the room, we weren't sure what to expect – an escape room in total darkness? What is that even like? Are we going to feel our way around a single room for an hour and try to manipulate shape-like puzzles? We were surprised when we discovered what it entailed! We found ourselves clambering through ropes, climbing up a rock wall, crawling through tunnels, smelling weird smells, sliding into a foam pit, and having to climb up into more tunnels.

While this would end up being one of the best escape rooms we have been in, primarily due to its originality, it ended up teaching us many lessons on managing our emotions and our perceptions. With this experience, we found light in the darkness - our first lesson involved how perception can affect our experiences. We weren't quite sure what to expect; however, we did have some ideas, and they were blown away the second we stepped in there. These expectations affected our sense of time (it felt like we were there for hours) because we kept finding new tunnels and rooms, and since we couldn't see what was ahead of us, we didn't know how much farther we needed to travel.

Another lesson was that of managing our emotions in a seemingly critical situation. There were times when we were crawling through a tunnel which suddenly became blocked (mild panic attack); others when it became sweltering (evidently we were crawling through a volcano); and yet again, when the tunnel started getting smaller and then even smaller (cue second mild panic attack). The main lesson for life is this: trust yourself to get through it, persist through the discomfort, and keep moving forward – even if you can't see the path in front of you. You'll know what you need to know when you need to know it.

Reflections

1. In what situations have you found light in the darkness?
2. What lessons have you learned from "dark" situations in your life?
3. How has stretching your comfort zone and doing "uncomfortable" things helped in your learning?

Lesson #18: Don't Quit!

In the escape room enthusiast world, we find that many individuals will keep a log of how many rooms they've done and of those, how many they have successfully escaped. Of course, we've seen some people keep much more detailed and varied statistics, but the most common numbers thrown around are the number of rooms one has completed and the percentage of those that were "successful" experiences. We, too, love to keep track of our rooms and are proud to have maintained a 97% escape rate.

There is a satisfaction to walking into a room, solving all of the challenges, and then escaping before the time ends. A successful escape doesn't always happen, which, of course, makes the "wins" that much more satisfying. There have been several occasions when it appeared we weren't going to make it out of a room. This sparks an overabundance of thoughts as one looks at the remaining time, compares it to what is believed to be left, and, depending on mood and level of fatigue, can lead to a desire to give up.

These moments of wondering if we will make it out of the room are great learning opportunities. In most cases, we use it to motivate ourselves to push forward and work until the bitter end. We've escaped with seconds on the timer, even from one room with two seconds left!

This same feeling of uncertainty happens a lot in life as well. We have something we want, perhaps a promotion, a goal we desire, or another challenge we're facing, and we're not sure we'll be able to accomplish it. We're facing a deadline and an overabundance of thoughts that we're not going to make it drives us to a desire to give up. It is precisely this time that we need to turn that feeling into motivation to see the challenge through – to move forward until the time is up.

Reflections

1. Reflect on a recent time that you wanted to give up; what did you do?
2. What can you learn from the action you took?
3. How can you train yourself to turn the feeling of uncertainty into motivation to keep pushing forward?

Lesson #19: Egos Aside, Always Double-Check

We had found Atlantis! Following in the footsteps of a world-famous explorer, we were in the temple of the Olympic God of the Sea. Deep within the secret chamber, we were looking for the ultimate source of power, but he wasn't going to make it easy. He had the denizens of the sea working for him, and we had to coax them into the necessary arrangement to open his inner sanctum. Our junior explorer, being great with animals, had matched the glowing colors of the sea fish, but the door would not open. It was time for help. Retracing the patterns, we realized that one of the sneaky little clownfish had tricked us.

When working on projects, we sometimes become either too close to notice or too trusting in ourselves to look at the problem with fresh eyes. Sometimes, it just takes another's touch to get it to work. We have learned not to take the offer of help, or the need for it, personally. One of the best indicators of a true expert is the recognition that sometimes we get things wrong – pobody's nerfect (I mean nobody's perfect!).

In escape rooms, it is so common that a lock won't work for one person, but will work for another (even using the same correct code) that we say "double-check," and our teammate will try it again with the same code. How you hold the lock, how the numbers line up, and whether you are pressing with just the right amount of pressure on the shackle can make the difference in whether a lock opens.

The same is true for many other things in life. Have you ever tried to convince someone of something, and with a single comment, another person sways them almost immediately? It is important to set egos aside and always have someone double-check your work or provide you with a different perspective. Each individual has something to contribute, and sometimes it takes a team effort no matter what.

Reflections

1. When you have a problem, at what point do you ask for help? In what cases would you wait to ask for help, and why?
2. How often do you have someone look over your work?
3. How can you implement a strategy to set egos aside and double-check when necessary in the future?

Lesson #20: Use The Goldilocks Principle

We "woke up" in a dark tiled room handcuffed to each other in a line and to a shackle on the wall. A staticky monitor came to life, and a strange voice ordered us to complete the puzzles around the room before he released deadly gas on us in 60 minutes. Our team had to work together to stretch out far enough to pass water from a toilet to float a handcuff key out of a narrow pipe. Surprisingly, only one of us had never been handcuffed with a murderous psychopath trying to kill us (he didn't get out much). As we freed ourselves from the restraints and started to work towards our escape, his nervousness came out as a steady stream of consciousness dialog. As we tried to pass information back and forth on related clues and puzzles, he continuously made comments on the history of things, interrupted other kidnapped victims, and worked puzzles out loud. In the end, we decided not to leave him in the room when we escaped, but it was a close one.

To understand the Goldilocks Principle, one must be familiar with the story of *Goldilocks and the Three Bears* (we recommend Googling it if you are not familiar with the story). Essentially, the principle, when used in this way, relates to ensuring that you are communicating just the right amount – not too little and not too much. When working as a team, there is such a thing as too much communication. If in doubt, use the WAIT test, "Why Am I Talking?" Sending and receiving information comes at an opportunity cost to both the sender and the receiver. Ask yourself, "Is the information I'm providing helping the other person or the task at hand, or is it something that can be saved for another moment (or not at all)?" Nervous talking and talking-to-think can become counterproductive. If you find that you are doing the vast majority of the talking when you are attempting to communicate with a person or group, ask yourself, "Am I giving them a chance to respond? Am I preventing them from providing input or asking needed questions?"

Likewise, not communicating enough can also become a problem. If you have information that is relevant and important, or you don't understand something, use the WAIT test a little differently: "Why Aren't I Talking?" Sometimes, anxiety or the worry that you might be judged prevents you from providing insightful and needed information.

Reflections

1. In general, do you use the Goldilock's Principle of Communication? What is your reasoning behind this belief?
2. When not using this principle, is your tendency to over-communicate or under-communicate? How can you notice when you are doing it?
3. What strategies can you put in place to ensure that you are communicating the right amount of information in the future?

Pro Tip #2: Dominoes And Morse Code

If it looks like a duck, swims like a duck, and quacks like a duck, then it probably is a duck.
—*Duck Test (Wikipedia)*

There are two variations of puzzles that pop up a lot across the many escape rooms we've done, and it's worth knowing a little about them. They are braille and morse code. We've noticed that frequently braille is used to communicate *without* sound, and morse code is used to communicate *with* sound. However, morse code can appear in many ways, such as a series of printed shapes or along with a note.

According to Wikipedia, braille was based upon a tactile military code called night writing that allowed soldiers to communicate silently without light. It is composed of a series of raised dots in a two by three grid (although there is a two by four variation). Because of its simplicity, it becomes a great method for communicating clues through a variety of methods (dominoes, nails in an arrangement, window panes, tiles, etc.) and is frequently used when the clue is out of sight (on the inside of a compartment, on the back of an immovable object, etc.). Remember with braille that the first ten letters of the alphabet are also used for the digits 1-9 and 0 (makes for fun when translating things). Also, numbers only use the top four dots.

A/1	B/2	C/3	D/4	E/5	F/6	G/7	H/8	I/9	J/0

K	L	M	N	O	P	Q	R	S	T

U	V	X	Y	Z

Each row is the same as the row above but with one extra raised dot. "W" was added late.

W

The other thing that we've seen used inventively is morse code. Sometimes you use an actual morse code machine, but many times it is more subtle through tapping in the wall, a bird calling, lights flashing, etc. Remember that we frequently come to rely on our eyes when we are frustrated or overly focused on a task, so keep those other senses open. With morse code, each letter is composed of up to four dots and dashes. The most common letters have less. Numbers are always composed of exactly five dots or dashes. A tip for using a morse code machine is that a dash is "3 units" long. When pressing the knob for a dash, count to three in your head quickly.

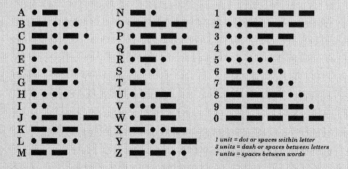

1 unit = dot or spaces within letter
3 units = dash or spaces between letters
7 units = spaces between words

Lesson #21: Overthinking (Don't Do It)

Time was running out. We had searched through the local market and could not find the missing field agent. The noise and colors of the Moroccan bazaar flooded our senses and made the hunt almost impossible. As our nervousness grew, we started seeing shapes in the herbs and grains, in the multitude of sandals for sale, and the variety of bags and garments. However, it was not the bags that proved important, but the levers and compartments behind them. Our entrance was revealed! And, the hidden elevator into the nuclear bunker was found. We were on our way to preventing a nuclear war.

Pareidolia is the term for when insignificant stimuli are perceived as significant. This often happens with frustration and fatigue, and that's when rational thought goes out the window. Wikipedia says that it can be considered a subset of *apophenia*, or the mistaken perception of a relationship between unrelated things. Basically, in heightened situations, we can all start to overthink and attempt to assign connections where they don't exist.

When we look for something, our minds want to shape reality so that we find what we're looking for. This is called *pattern recognition* and describes the cognitive process for relating inputs with prior experience. With a lot of stimuli or heightened emotional context, this can cause us to assume that everything has a meaning or is significant, even when it's not.

Have you ever had an interaction with your boss, a coworker, or spouse and thought to yourself, "She/He is mad at me." Only to later find out that they were absorbed with another issue altogether? It had nothing to do with you, but you were trying to ascribe meaning to each little comment, facial expression, or nuance.

In an escape room, this can translate to time lost and unnecessary work. In other life situations, it can morph into angst, worry, miscommunication, and loss of productivity.

Reflections

1. Do you overthink little details of interactions with others? Do you ask for clarification, or do you dwell on it?
2. Are you sensitive to the small comments or facial expressions you make? Could these be misread as meaning more to someone else?
3. What is the story you've built up in your mind about what someone else is thinking? Have you considered the impact of those stories?

Lesson #22: Whoa! No One Said There'd Be Math!

The body count was rising, and the hunt was on. Deep within the dark forest, the once-revered geneticist had devolved into a vengeful shell of a man and was releasing human-animal hybrids into a quiet village. Our team had stumbled upon his cabin lab, and were trying to analyze the scrawling formulas written across the walls and ceiling. If the hybrid monsters hounding us weren't bad enough, he had used math in his equations! Luckily, it was a "simple" substitution problem, and the antidote for his were-creatures was found.

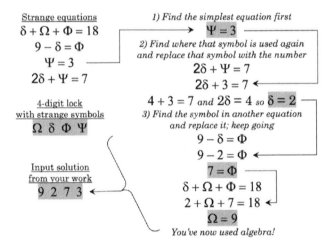

Our high school math teacher was right; we need math (in this case, algebra) in real life! But, for those of you that don't find yourselves in this kind of situation very often, there are still a variety of uses for reasoning and math in other parts of our lives. Reasoning, logic, deduction, analysis, and comparison are all offshoots of math.

Additionally, many studies are associating the mental health benefits of playing games and solving puzzles. A 2017 study by researchers at the University of Manchester found that video games combining physical activity and cognitively-demanding tasks (sounds like an escape room) improve cognitive functioning. Reduced cognitive functioning can be a precursor to Alzheimer's disease and dementia. Keeping our brains engaged is important (yes, you need to use your brain every once in a while).

Even if you don't do escape rooms as an obsession, there are a variety of apps and games to give your gray matter a workout.

Reflections

1. What are some games you can use to help you work on your logic and reasoning abilities?
2. What aspects of your life involve observation and deduction? Do you feel that your cognitive abilities are as sharp as they once were?
3. What are some additional easy strategies you can implement to improve your mental health?

Lesson #23: Ask For A Clue For #$@*'s Sake!

For this adventure, an insane dentist locked us in his dental clinic. We had to uncover clues located throughout the room to liberate ourselves before we became his next victims. As soon as we entered the room, several team members narrowed their focus to decipher a code they found in a sink (after we drained a pool of blood from it). Since it involved math and a substitution code, they began diligently working on it in an attempt to open a nearby lock.

The other team members, who prefer not to do math, continued searching throughout the room. One team member found several clues concerning the substitution part of the sink formula but couldn't quite make the connection as to how it could help. The team member working on the sink clue was so focused, they could not be torn away to help figure out how they were related.

After asking for a clue from the game master, the team was able to find the missing connection in how the clue related to the formula in the sink and was able to decipher the code for the lock quickly. Finally, after ten minutes in the room, we were making progress.

How often do we get faced with a problem in life, and we completely focus on how it needs to be solved, even if it doesn't appear that we may have all of the necessary information? We become tunnel-focused on the problem in front of us, neglecting to look at other possible creative solutions for working through a challenge. And here is the kicker – we don't ask for help. If we had asked for help from the game master earlier in the experience, we would not have wasted the first ten minutes of our experience.

See *Pro Tip #4* about how important it is to ask for clues when you need them.

Reflections

1. Where are you stuck in your life right now?
2. Who could you ask for help in becoming unstuck?
3. How will you ask this person to help you? (What will you say? When will you ask?)

Lesson #24: Double-Tap (Know Your Tools)

We had been coaxed into an underworld job in early 1900s London. Our employer was hooded and wouldn't reveal the details of the job until we met face-to-face. When we arrived, there was no sign of the mysterious bloke who hired us – only a note with instructions. As instructed, we descended into the dark cellar with only candles to light our way. We were stopped in our tracks when we saw a bloody name scrawled on the iron-bound door. Ignoring the ominous implications, we entered the basement and beheld a virtual museum of ancient artifacts, boxes, and chests. A quick casing of the room revealed almost 40 locks of various sizes and types. Our work was cut out for us. It was a good thing we were experienced larcenists, or the locks would have stopped us in our tracks. There were locks with no keyholes, locks requiring a pin-like key, and one we luckily had seen during another drudgery that was shaped like a fish (there was something about that fish's eye).

Learning about locks and how they work is a fun aspect of escape rooms. One of the most common locks we see is the directional lock, a type of lock opened by pressing a pad on the front of the lock in various directions. The trick with directional locks is that they need to be reset before attempting to put in a new code. Resetting the lock is done by pressing down twice on the shackle, also known as the "double-tap." Before we came to know this tool well, there were many times we've entered a code and then pressed down on the shackle resetting it (and therefore not opening the lock).

Using the right tool for the right job is important. For instance, did you know that golfers use the same swing no matter which club they are using? To change the outcome, they change the club, not their swing. The same metaphor can be used when choosing our other tools in life. Do you use the same tone of voice for your children as you use on your colleagues at work? For your boss or your spouse? Do you expect the same results?

In life, one of the most important things is knowing your tools and how to use them. Remember, your toolbox includes more than just physical things. It includes things like soft-skills, technical skills, insights, experiences, and communication skills (and how to use those computer and phone apps). In *Outliers: The Story of Success*, Malcolm Gladwell suggests that it takes 10,000 hours of deliberate practice in a specific task to master it. While we might never reach the 10,000-hour level for all of our tools, our skills, knowledge, and abilities must be frequently tested, augmented, and strengthened. When you need to use one of your "tools" at a critical time (for example, that big presentation), it is too late to practice.

Sometimes referred to as lifelong learning, continuous learning, or self-improvement, the need to keep your tools sharp is important in ALL aspects of your life.

Reflections

1. What was the last book you read on self-improvement? How long ago did you read it?
2. How often do you deliberately work on improving yourself? Do you stick with it longer than a New Year's resolution?
3. What one thing would you like to improve? Think of three ways that you could work on it today.

Lesson #25: Using Force Only Works In Star Wars

Before every escape room, the game master gives a brief on the rules and mission. Every time we hear some variation of the "no force is necessary" rule, usually explained by saying if we have to use more than two fingers to move it, it probably shouldn't be moved until we find a code to open it. It is interesting to think that people so frequently and quickly resort to physical force to attain their goals, from moving or shaking things to unscrewing or disassembling, and even to outright breaking things. While in an escape room, this can be annoying to other players, counterproductive, and even result in the room becoming out of service, spoiling the fun for everyone.

In an escape room, resorting to force frequently happens because people are frustrated or intellectually lazy – "I can't figure it out, but I'm sure I could break it open." Aside from never needing to use force in an escape room, using force creates a negative environment and fails to recognize the spirit of the game. It also tends to happen more when people don't want to ask for help (ask for help, for #$@*'s sake).

The equivalent in life to using force comes when people try to make things happen. They may want to control the outcome of a specific project and push everyone involved to complete their work a certain way. It could be that one has a goal in mind and a specific way they believe they should go about obtaining it, so they try to force people and circumstances in their life to fit within their idea of how they should accomplish the goal. When we attempt to force things to be or go a certain way, we are not open to the possibilities of getting the outcome we desire in a different (and often more effective) way.

Reflections

1. When assigning a task to another person, do you also tell them exactly how they need to accomplish it? How do they tend to respond?
2. What causes you to want to use force?
3. What are some strategies you can use to ensure you are not using force to get to the outcome you wish to achieve?

Lesson #26: What's The Rush?

Before each escape room experience, the game master will brief the participants on the rules of the room, go over the story behind the mission, and provide guidelines for making the "leader board." The leader board is a ranking of teams that have made it out of the room with the fastest times. Some escape room locations require you to complete the room without any clues with the fastest time; others limit the number of clues you are allowed if you want to make it on the leader board; while others go by only the fastest times. We usually tell the game master that we don't need the guidelines for the leader board because we want to enjoy the experience as much as possible, not rushing it, but still meeting the challenge of the room's mission within the allotted time.

Unfortunately, in one of our experiences, we were teamed up with very competitive (and highly intoxicated) strangers. This unpleasant experience was in our first year of training as escapeletes, and we hadn't quite mastered the ability to schedule to increase our chances of being in a private room. As the game master was briefing us on our mission – apprentices that needed to locate a missing wizard (he disappeared and left his spellbook behind, so we were quite sure his disappearance was for nefarious reasons) – the others started searching through the room while one woman started dividing up pages of the spellbook between her teammates. They were completely ignoring the game master while we tried to listen to the briefing politely.

Twenty minutes later, after a whirlwind of bodies moved throughout the fairly small room, we had found the wizard (he got stuck in the mirror of all places!).

Our "team" made the leader board, and we were stuck wondering what we had just experienced. We had four people in our little team, so we spent $120 for a 20-minute experience – which translated into watching a total of eight people walk around in a room and yell at each other about various clues and puzzles.

When we set a goal in life and rush to accomplish it, we are doing ourselves an injustice because it's all about the process of achieving the goal. The growth in an individual happens while they are becoming who they need to become to accomplish the goal.

Reflections

1. What areas of your life are you rushing through?
2. How can you ensure that you are focusing on the process of *becoming*, rather than solely on the outcome?
3. When setting a goal in the future, how will you make the process just as important as the outcome?

Lesson #27: Choose Your Team Wisely

We arrived at the office of Sherlock Holmes. As his assistants, we knew something was off – he was not here, but there was still ice in his glass of scotch. We soon discovered that he got lost somewhere in time, and we only had 60 minutes to find him before he was lost forever.

We had an amazing team of assistant investigators. We knew this because we had carefully chosen our teammates for this particular adventure. We had two individuals who were excellent at deductive reasoning and paying attention to the details, and two individuals who could step back, see the big picture and use inductive reasoning very well. One was great at math and spatial logic, and another great at word scrambles and logic puzzles.

With our team members each taking puzzles that fit their strengths well, we were able to liberate Sherlock from being trapped in time before his ice fully melted. We celebrated our success by enjoying some food and beverage at the nearby pub.

In life, we need to choose who we surround ourselves with carefully. These individuals have the most influence in our lives, so they must be a positive influence on us. As a team, we should exceed the value of each person individually. The same goes for our professional teams. As much as we can, we need to choose who is on our team carefully – do everyone's strengths complement each other? Are the team members able to work well together?

Reflections

1. Who are the people on your "team" in life right now?
2. Are they the right people on your team for who you want to be in life?
3. How are you going to maximize your team (in life and at work)?

Lesson #28: Be Confident, Not Cocky

We had a great time at an escape room location in Malta, as the staff was extremely friendly and helpful. We were quite impressed that they had posted themed definitions around their facility including: "Over-Confidence: Most people who proclaim that they are the best at solving puzzles often turn out to be the ones who cannot see the most obvious things in the room. Everyone's contribution is precious!" So true!

Having completed hundreds of escape rooms, we find the more rooms we do, the more careful we need to be about assumptions and past experiences getting in the way. We also find that the cockiest of players (who've normally completed less than ten rooms) miss the most clues and are often surpassed by people doing their first or second rooms, especially children.

As one works toward mastery of a subject, skill, or ability, we find that the best lessons come from letdowns or setbacks. One can't truly master something without failures or losses because learning is a series of trial and error. Making mistakes is an essential part of getting better.

When approaching new things in life, be confident in your abilities while not assuming that you will never make mistakes or that you will always succeed. The journey is as much a part of the success as the goal.

Additionally, you never know who you might run into along the way. You might be playing an escape room with one of those people who have completed more than 1,000 rooms (yes, they are out there). Recognize that each person brings a unique set of skills, abilities, and experiences in each situation and should be treated with respect and fairness. They might notice the one thing at the exact right time that helps the team accomplish their goal.

Reflections

1. How do you ensure you see things with a beginner's mind?
2. Do you ask people for a "fresh set of eyes" on an issue? How does bringing in new ideas and new perspectives help improve outcomes?
3. When you become good at something, how can you ensure you are confident and not cocky?

Lesson #29: You Create Your Experience

Having done hundreds of escape rooms, we get excited about novel escape room experiences. For example, we enjoyed doing a room in complete darkness, liberating ourselves from an escape boat (yes – a real boat on the water), and even breaking out of a coffin (yes – a real coffin!). We were extremely excited about what we believed was going to be a room in complete silence.

When we first heard about the room, the story we created in our heads was that, as we tried to escape a space ship, we had to be completely silent, so as not to alert the aliens, who would attack if they heard us. We booked the room a month in advance of our weekend trip to the area. On the drive to the location, we discussed the best ways to tackle the room since one of us could be "quiet challenged" in the best of times (to be overly polite). Once we arrived, the game master led us to the space tube that would lead us onto the spaceship. As we waited in the tube for the door to open, with our anticipation building to a peak, we silently headed into the ship when the countdown timer began.

Very quickly, we realized that the "silent" part of the room only lasted until we solved the first clue, and the only consequence of making too much noise was the main lights shutting off, leaving us with the glow of the monitor to work on that first puzzle. We had built up the room so much in our heads that we were disappointed the experience didn't require complete silence the entire time. Here's the thing though – it was a really good room! The set-like quality of the spaceship and the logical flow of the puzzles were superb. If we hadn't created such a story about the room before we entered it, we wouldn't have been disappointed by only one aspect of it.

How often do we do this in life? We set up expectations about a person, a job, a vacation, or some other aspect in our life, and then we miss out on the experience because it didn't fit in with our expectations. Of course, we should have some expectations that should be met (such as we will not accept violence in any relationship); however, we are often over-inflating our expectations, and when others or experiences don't measure up to them, we allow ourselves to be disappointed and not see the person, or experience, for what it is bringing us. Where are you doing this in your life right now?

Reflections

1. Reflect on the last time you entered an experience with specific expectations.
2. How could you have adjusted your expectations to make the experience a better one for you?
3. How can you take this learning into setting your expectations for future experiences?

Lesson #30: Have An Awareness Of Subtext

Occasionally, instead of a game master, an escape room will have live actors in the room. This can be both fun and daunting. While it is fun to interact with actors in character, sometimes it becomes extremely difficult to get clues or help. This can be compounded if the group becomes distracted by the actor or the gameplay and stops focusing on the tasks.

A great example happened when we signed up for a serial killer/horror-themed room. We had been grouped with three other players who had never been in an escape room and thought they were going into a haunted house experience. Their expectations of the room became obvious when one of the players started screaming at every creak or bang in the background music, which was compounded by a constant medium volume static overlaying the music. In this escape room, there was no game master and no hints until you "saved" the trapped actor. However, the actor played a disoriented and crazed mental patient and would wander in and out of the different rooms, not giving straight answers to any questions. The "screamer" also thought the actor was there to scare her and would constantly stare at him and scream and run into other parts of the room.

After being distracted by this for an unuseful amount of time, we got into our rhythm and were working the puzzles (even with the screamer keeping up with her screaming). At one point, the actor walked by and loudly slammed a book down. At first, it appeared to be part of his character, but something seemed off. Picking up the book and looking through it, it became obvious that it was a needed part of the puzzle we were working on. Taking a moment to interpret the undertones and intent of the in-room actor became key. After realizing he wasn't just up to distracting antics, we examined why he slammed a book down next to us. He was trying to communicate without being explicit.

We experienced a similar situation with a live actor in a speakeasy-themed room. The actor was asking questions and providing seemingly deflecting answers. After a few times, we started to catch on to the hidden clues. When people communicate, we sometimes have to read the subtext (or what is not plainly being communicated), consider the perspective of the sender, and deduce what is meant. By the way, super kudos to all the great actor/game masters we've encountered!

We recently saw reading the subtext play out in a more serious situation. A woman had called 911 and was trying to order a pizza. The dispatcher at first thought it was a bogus call, but then started to listen to the way the caller responded. It turned out to be a domestic violence incident, and the woman was trying to get help but couldn't be more direct.

Reflections

1. Can you think of a time when you reflected on a conversation or situation and realized it could have been interpreted as something completely different?
2. Have you ever tried to communicate information to someone without being explicit? Did the recipient understand what you were trying to say? If not, why not?
3. How can you improve on your ability to read subtext?

Pro Tip #3: Scheduling and Getting Rooms

One of the challenges of playing escape rooms is interacting with others (even friends and family) and understanding people's strengths and blindspots. This is particularly challenging when you are playing with strangers (or in a large group). Being grouped with strangers in an escape room is a uniquely American practice. We were alerted to this when we played in Dublin and were talking with the owner. He also expressed his surprise that Americans take escape rates and leader boards very seriously. He said that if places in Ireland had escape rates below 20%, people would stop playing. Not to mention those places that pride themselves on escape rates below 10% (which we jokingly refer to as meaning that their puzzles are illogical).

Getting grouped with strangers is inevitable in most cases in the United States. Unless you are the type of player who prefers to do escape rooms with strangers or can afford to buy out the whole room (we tried, and it became way too expensive), here are a few suggestions on how to get a room to yourself:

1. Timing: playing early in the day (especially weekdays or Sunday mornings).
2. Avoid holidays: unless you have a large group that can block out the whole room.
3. Buy an extra: if a room accommodates only 5 or 6 people, and you are going with 2 or 3 (or even 4), buying one more can help block groups from having enough places to fit in with you. This doesn't keep the potential "singles" from joining but has worked for us to keep a room to ourselves.

4. Look for scaled pricing: some places will allow a smaller group to block out the room for a slight increase in cost (e.g., two people at $40 each, three people at $35, 4 people at $30, and so on). We like this variation and would like to see more of it in the U.S.

5. Groupons or special offers: many places allow for a greatly reduced price and a private room to advertise their location.

6. Play multiple rooms and ask: we've found that we have the best luck when we ask if we can get a room to ourselves. Of course, it helps when we're playing more than one room and build rapport with the owner, manager, or game master (who like to have their games appreciated by enthusiastic players). Being enthusiastic (and experienced) has gotten us into beta testing rooms. Shout out to those owners who have asked us to beta test their rooms!

In the end, playing with others can be fulfilling and educational. In all our rooms, we have only been grouped with three or four other teams that were bad experiences. Many times, we have helped others have a better first-time experience.

Lesson #31: Take Special Care In Large Teams

Unfortunately, our group of four got caught in a blizzard on what we thought was going to be a relaxing ski trip at a nice resort. We took shelter in a nearby cabin and were dismayed to find that six strangers had taken shelter in the same cabin. We found ourselves locked in a cabin with ten people (a cabin that should not have been able to hold ten people), and we only had 60 minutes to escape it before an avalanche destroyed the cabin.

It was very hard to move about the cabin with so many people in it, which added to the frustration of the attempt to liberate ourselves. Not only was there not enough space for the larger group, but it was also quite disorganized in getting everyone to work together in advancing our escape efforts. We split up into smaller groups to work on various challenges, but voices would get lost in the mix as individuals tried to communicate collaboratively.

Luckily, we were able to work together enough to escape seconds before the avalanche demolished the cabin, all of us leaving exhausted from the extra effort of working with a large team in such a chaotic and disorganized manner.

When we work in large teams in life – professionally or personally – this reminds us how important it is to take time as a team to discuss how we will work together, what ground rules we will set as a team, and ways we can remain organized and make sure everyone's voice is heard.

Reflections

1. As a team member of a large team (personally or professionally), what do you do to ensure the team works together well?
2. What can you do better or differently to ensure the team works together well?
3. How will you change how you approach working with a larger team in the future?

Lesson #32: Plan And Adapt

One thing we like to do before going into an escape room is to plan how we will divide and conquer. If it's just the two of us, the planning takes less time and effort in many ways (mostly because through experience, we have an inherent plan). However, as the group or the task grows, planning becomes an essential aspect of success. From the first decision about how the group will be broken up, to knowing our strengths and being ready to switch puzzles and tasks quickly, a bit of planning goes a long way.

As the Prussian Field Marshall, Helmuth von Moltke, said, no plan survives first contact with the enemy, so planning and then being ready to adapt is essential. We frequently find ourselves having to work a puzzle or task we don't like, or we can't make a lock work right, and need another person to try. We must always be ready to assume another role or tackle something outside of our comfort zone.

In life, depending on the task and team members, planning can be easy. A general alignment of skills and personality with a role can take only a few moments. From the simple "pick teams" to a more involved "each team will have one expert in each area," taking the time to plan out beforehand will ensure the best chance of success. In the most chaotic of circumstances (we like to refer to those cases as "peewee soccer"), we can pick a manager or someone to pull the team together. Leaders can also keep the team aligned with the mission of the overall group.

As the task progresses, we can then adapt our plan to the changing circumstances. In escape rooms, we've had times when we thought we would team up a certain way, but then the teams organically realigned unexpectedly and more naturally. Remember, we are all made up of a range of personalities, skills, and abilities. It is natural for us to be working one end of a spectrum (for example, being extroverted) on a given day, even if it is different from our dominant personality (being introverted). Just go with the flow and work with the energy you're feeling at the time.

Reflections

1. Do you like to plan or go in and "wing it?" Do you plan for certain jobs and adapt to others?
2. Are you always the same role on a team? Are you able to adapt and take on a role outside your comfort zone?
3. What are the strengths and weaknesses of your teammates? Do you expect a certain individual to always do a certain task? Do you help others develop by giving them a chance at a new task?

Lesson #33: The Leader Creates The Weather

We were on day two of a six-day escapecation and were excited to have a day full of fun escape rooms (nine total!). The first three escapes were quite fun – locked in yet another serial killer's lair, trapped on yet another cursed pirate ship, and locked in yet another jail. For the fourth escape, we got caught in another spaceship, attempting to break free of our captivity before the aliens made their way into the ship. This escape was fun – until it wasn't. As our group gathered to focus on one puzzle, one of our team members flipped a switch, and an access panel opened up. This allowed us to bypass the puzzle and gave us access to a clue for the next puzzle.

We continued on our way but, near the end, noticed that there were only a few minutes left on the timer. Something seemed off. We had three minutes to decipher a control panel map and put the right colored electrical cords into their respective places on the panel. We got to the last wire, and the buzzer went off – aliens began to invade the ship, and we didn't escape on time. When the game master came in (our "leader" helping us through the process), we found that he had taken six minutes away from our time because we "cheated" by flipping the switch to open the access panel. The entire team was livid that our game master (1) thought we were cheating when that was not the intention at all, and (2) punished us without any discussion (not to mention we paid $30 a person to play the game). Emotions were high, and even though we had three previous great escapes at the location, we vowed never to go back and left an unfavorable review.

After a lunch break allowing us to relax and recover from the incident, we found ourselves on our fifth escape that day – in a bargain basement. The idea was so novel; we don't remember what the mission was - we were having fun solving all the puzzles. At one point, we thought we were supposed to use an object to get into the manager's business office, and it worked, so we kept going. The game master later explained that was not what the tool was supposed to be used for but that he was "not going to discipline innovative ideas," so he let us keep going. We left this location feeling very satisfied that we were able to accomplish our mission and motivated to get to the next site for our remaining escape attempts.

The leaders (game masters) in both of these situations behaved quite differently from each other, which had a tremendous effect on each of their team's motivation. The leader "makes the weather" for the team – as a leader, is it sunny and productive in your neck of the woods, or is it stormy and demotivating?

Reflections

1. Whether an informal or a formal leader, you make the weather for others. What type of weather do you generally make?
2. How can you ensure you're making sunny and productive weather for your team?
3. What are some strategies to turn a storm into a sunny summer day for your team?

Lesson #34: Relationship First

For this family adventure that we chose to do on Christmas Eve, dressed in ugly sweaters, we were a team of paranormal investigators. A little girl had gone missing a couple of years before, and her parents had noticed weird things happening in her room, therefore calling us in to investigate. We only had 60 minutes to complete our mission before the ghosts took over the room.

We worked very well as a team, uncovering clues and finding more and more sinister explanations for the little girl's disappearance. We were able to make it into a secret room that held even more paranormal clues. Most of the team was having fun, enjoying spending time with each other while making progress in the investigation and responding to the scary aspects of the experience (what's a few screams here and there?). One team member, however, was very focused on the investigation and was getting frustrated if there was any perceived lack of focus on the mission.

The difference in team member moods became distinctly apparent when another "jump scare" presented itself, leading two team members to jump back and scream. The focused team member rolled their eyes and pushed past the others to grab the clue produced from the scary event. A "jump scare" is a moment in an escape room when something or someone pops out, making the participants jump because it scares them.

It was that moment we stopped our investigation and reminded everyone that it was Christmas Eve, and we are doing this as a family to enjoy our time together. Our goal was not to complete the investigation in the allotted time, rather the goal of our mission was to build our relationship as a family by doing something that we enjoyed together. This moment of pausing to remind ourselves that our purpose was "relationship first" helped bring everyone back together as a team, and we finished our mission 20 minutes early! As a result, anytime we have a moment where one team member gets a bit too focused on the mission, all another team member has to utter is "relationship first" to remind them why we are engaging in these escape experiences.

In life, both personally and professionally, we can get laser-focused on going after our goals: sometimes so much that we forget to both enjoy the process of achieving that goal and making sure that we nurture the relationships in our lives. When we reach the end of our days, we won't regret whether we achieved a certain goal or not. What we will regret are the relationships we neglected or even lost along the way because we did not nurture them.

Reflections

1. How do you handle the challenges that you face?
2. Are you ensuring that your relationships come first before the mission?
3. How can you keep your relationships (personal and professional) as a priority when going after your goals?

Lesson #35: Revisit The Past

We should have known that opening a cursed book would lead to trouble, but who would have guessed that the magical tome would transport us from the professor's study to a haunted ship 100 years in the past? Finding the lost token on the creaky ship had been challenging, but what do we do with it now? We searched the ship high and low and couldn't figure it out. Suddenly, it dawned on us - the book. Rushing back through the portal, we returned to the professor's study. Placing the token on the correct mark in the book and repeating the incantation released the tormented evil and saved us from the same doom.

In many escape rooms, we assume that once something is used or we have moved away from it, then we won't need to use it again. However, sometimes you have to go back to the beginning, or an earlier point, and use something from the current room to solve a past problem or use a previous tool to help solve the current problem.

In life, revisiting past solutions or applying new knowledge to old problems can help us develop as individuals and improve current performance. In the work environment, institutional knowledge and experience are valuable tools. And, who hasn't heard "getting back to the basics" or "those who ignore history are doomed to repeat it?" Not all problems need a "new" solution.

Additionally, as we grow and develop, there are benefits to examining past experiences and problems with a fresh set of perspectives and experiences. Would we react today the same way we would've reacted ten years ago? Can we use old solutions for new problems or new solutions for old problems? Has time and experience changed us?

Reflections

1. How would you address an old problem today? What would you do differently?
2. How would you have addressed a problem today with a ten-year younger you?
3. When stuck, do you ever "go back to the beginning" to work through it again? If not, consider doing so next time you're stuck.

Lesson #36: Get Organized

In an escape room, staying organized is key (pun intended). There are two rookie mistakes that many players make: picking up solved puzzles and working on them because a player doesn't know the puzzle has been completed and moving clues around the room in a way that disconnects them from their purpose. The first type happens when the rooms are crowded, and people aren't communicating or listening well. The second type happens when players want to pile all their clues into a single spot (either to control them or in an attempt to look at everything at once).

We normally try to keep clues where we found them, especially since their initial position could be a clue in and of itself. Then once a clue or puzzle is complete, we will set them aside in a designated spot that everyone knows is for completed items. We try to keep keys in the locks they opened at the place where the lock was originally located. This also helps the game master in resetting the room (which is the polite way to play).

When trying to get organized, less is more. A complex plan for organizing clues or puzzles can be more trouble than it is worth. Likewise, as players get engrossed in the room, they become focused on their tasks and can easily forget a complicated plan.

In the work environment, simple understood organizing principles (e.g., where we keep files and references) can reduce stress and ensure that everyone is sharing and communicating information. In our personal lives, consistent and agreed upon arrangements can save us from decision fatigue (we only have so much mental energy each day – let's save it for the important stuff).

Reflections

1. What aspects of your life are organized? What aspect is not organized?
2. Do you ever have to redo the work that was completed because you can't find it? Would that time have been better spent investing in a little organization?
3. For your next big task (personal or professional), how will you be even more organized to tackle it effectively?

Lesson #37: Look Within First

In an undisclosed location in Europe, we had the pleasure of beta-testing a new escape room. Beta-testing means that the room was not yet open to the general public as they were testing out the different puzzles and tech in the room; in particular, they wanted to see how it translated for English speaking escapees. In this room, like in several others we've done, the players are split up at the beginning, with one of us locked in a cage. In the past, when one player is locked up, we make it our number one goal on working to free the participant, attempting to ignore any puzzles that don't appear to progress towards that goal.

The participant initially locked in the cage (names will not be shared to protect the guilty) did a quick scan of the area within the enclosure to see if there was anything that could help towards gaining their freedom. Not finding anything, they then focused their attention outside of the cell, helping the other participant to uncover clues to open the cage. The attempt to open the cage went on for more than five minutes until a technical issue led to the game master resetting the game. During the reset, participants switched places so that the initially caged escapee could do a "better job" of searching. In less than a minute, the newly trapped participant found a map in the cell that helped quickly gain their freedom.

The main lesson learned in this experience, especially for the initially caged escapelete, is to look within first for the answers. We are so quick to look externally to solve problems (or to blame others for our problems not getting solved), that we forget to look at ourselves first.

Reflections

1. Reflect on where you feel "trapped" in life and examine what role you play in that feeling.
2. When coming upon an obstacle in life, is your first instinct to look to external reasons for it being present? How can you change this?
3. What are some ways you can train yourself to look both internally and externally when solving problems in your life?

Lesson #38: Build Rapport Quickly

The next challenge we had to face was ridding our family of an ancient curse that was growing in power and would soon wreak havoc on our remaining family members. We weren't sure if we were up for the challenge because earlier that morning we had escaped a shipwreck, uncovered a dastardly secret experiment on humans, and located ghosts in an old hotel to release them into the light, and then we drove four hours to fight off our family's curse. It was a busy day saving the world!

We like interacting with people as a general rule, but for this particular challenge, we knew we would need to have an engaged game master to help us accomplish our mission, so it would be especially important to interact with him before we began the experience. As soon as we arrived on site, we began getting to know our game master, who turned out to be a pretty funny guy. As we went about our tasks, he not only provided quite a few laughs, but he also guided us when we got sluggish from the long day. With our game master's help, we were able to thwart the evil entity that had put a curse on our family. We are all now living happily and healthy due to our efforts.

It is not only because it is the right thing to do with our fellow human beings, but building rapport is an important skill to have and easy to do if you become genuinely interested in others. Building rapport will help you work better on teams, get or give better customer service, and make life a little easier as others are more willing to help you accomplish your goals. Do you take the time to build rapport with those around you? If not, you never know what could come out of a simple conversation – a new job, a new friend, and many other potential opportunities.

Reflections

1. In what ways are you building rapport with those around you?
2. How can you build rapport more quickly with others?
3. In what areas of rapport building do you need to improve, and how will you work on them?

Lesson #39: Stay Positive!

Based on our experiences, we created another rule for our escapelete team – don't enter a room in a bad mood. Not only does it ruin the experience for all those involved, but it also greatly limits our ability to engage in creative problem-solving, which is a requirement for successful escape experiences.

As a team, we've developed signals we can give each other when one appears to be succumbing to a bad mood. If it is before we enter a room, we discuss what would best help the other move into a more positive frame of mind. We also have a signal if a bad mood appears while in the middle of an escape experience. We have both developed our own strategies for moving into a more positive frame of mind as quickly as possible when given the signal. Sometimes it is pausing for a moment to do a breathing exercise, while other times it is taking a break and working on something else until the mood passes.

Let's apply this to life. To thrive in life, you need to experience positive emotions at least five times more often than negative emotions. According to numerous research studies, five-to-one is the magic ratio. In Maureen Gaffney's book, *Flourishing*, she makes a good case for how much positive emotions play a part in our ability to thrive in life. She states that positive emotions broaden, build, and transform us.

When you experience a positive emotion, it puts you in a more receptive state of mind, triggering patterns of thought that are more flexible, creative, and adaptable. These are the thought patterns you need to achieve your desires more quickly. The good news is that if you have a natural inclination toward the negative, with deliberate effort and practice, you can build up the positive and reduce the negative.

Reflections

1. What is your positive-to-negative emotion ratio?
2. How can you ensure you are in a positive frame of mind before going after a challenge?
3. What are some healthy ways you can process your negative emotions so that you can move through them more quickly?

Lesson #40: Break Free Of Your Constraints

We found ourselves trapped in a carnival this time – one where many children had gone missing over the last thirty years. Our team was tasked with uncovering the individual behind the disappearances and bringing him or her to justice. We had fun playing several of the carnival games to find different clues bringing us closer to gaining access to the ringmaster's tent, which we believed would help us uncover who was responsible for the disappearances.

Unfortunately, we got stumped on the shooting gallery game. We had to shoot a laser into targets quickly to get certain numbers to light up. There were lines on the floor that the shooter could choose to shoot from, each labeled based on the difficulty level: hard, medium, easy. One player started at the medium line and did not beat the game. Another player tried the easy line and could not beat the game. Finally, another player, who did not allow himself to be bound by assumed constraints, took the gun directly up to the target and shot the laser into each of the required holes quickly and easily. We gained access to the ringmaster's tent and discovered the perpetrator soon after that.

We often allow assumed constraints to limit how we experience life. Assumed constraints are simply beliefs that limit our experience. Because we saw the lines on the floor, we believed we had to stand behind them to shoot the targets. How often are we doing this to ourselves in life? We believe we must play by a certain set of rules, but do we? We're not referring to breaking laws or our organization's rules; however, we often come up with constraints that hold us back, not even realizing that they are rules we created.

Reflections

1. In what areas of your life are you limiting yourself based on your assumed constraints?
2. How can you look past those limitations to help you expand how you tackle the issue?
3. How can you train yourself to break free of your assumptions in the future?

Pro Tip #4: Asking For Help

Asking for help from the game master is a surprisingly contentious issue among the many escapees with whom we've interacted. Some purists feel that asking for help somehow makes the rooms too easy or is not in the spirit of the game. Or, those who are shooting for leader boards can be very adamant about not getting help (many leader boards either require having received no clues or a very limited number).

Our advice to other escapees is to ask for help! If given a choice between swallowing one's pride and asking for help or not getting out of a room, we always take the former. Our philosophy is that the owners and game designers have taken a lot of time and effort to build their game, and we want to see all of it. We want to get to the end (in fact, we shoot for having a few minutes to a few seconds remaining when we get out).

Our advice on getting clues in a room is to work diligently for five minutes (of a 60-minute room), and if you are still stumped, ask for a clue. We find that the first clue helps us understand the game designer and normally starts a cascade of a better understanding of the remaining puzzles. If you are playing competitively and have a room with the standard three clue policy, use one early, keep one for the last five minutes, and then use the other as strategically as possible. While we seldon get on the leader boards (and never intentionally try for them), our escape rate of more than 97% means that we are having fun and enjoying all the hard work put in by the game designers.

Interestingly, when observing people who don't want help, it is very reminiscent of watching people struggle in other aspects of their lives. Since when has asking for help been a bad thing? If you saw someone doing something completely wrong, would you step up and help? Should they be brave enough to ask for help? In many ways, we believe that this philosophy helps us break down the stigma of asking for help.

On a different note, in addition to competitive players, there are also competitive establishments (mostly in the U.S.) that take their games very seriously (maybe a little too seriously). Some of these locations take time away for each clue! There is a "legal" argument that paying for 60 minutes means players should get 60 minutes (unless otherwise noted in the location's legal terms). To those establishments out there that have this practice, our suggestion is to add time to completion rates with a real 60-minute limit, rather than shortening the experience.

Lesson #41: Failure Is A Great Teacher

There were three of us locked in an asylum doctor's office. The mad doctor was performing dark experiments on the patients before a mysterious fire closed the asylum, and our team was tasked with investigating this claim in the now-abandoned asylum. We quickly searched the office and found several clues as to the doctor's mad experiments, including some weird tools and medical equipment hidden within the walls.

At one point in our investigation, we noticed there were pictures of previous asylum directors on the wall, along with their dates of directorship. It was odd that they were looking in all different directions in their photos. Then we found a directional lock, and it all made sense. As noted in a previous chapter, a directional lock is a lock that uses directional inputs as the combination. It allows for the slide button to be pushed up, down, left, and right, in a certain combination to unlock it. We input the directions that the director's eyes were looking in each of the eight portraits from left to right along the wall. The lock didn't open.

Since we have a rule of always double-checking each other, we had another team member try the same combination sequence without success. Both team members shared their theories for how to proceed, one believing that we should input it by the chronological date that the directors held the directorship, and the other arguing for another way to try the lock (friendly arguing, of course). The first team member arguing for the chronological order felt very strongly that this was the correct combination (why else would they include dates of directorship?). However, since the second teammate felt just as strongly about their solution, the discussion was ended, and the second teammate had an opportunity to test their theory. When it didn't work out, they tried the chronological combination, and it worked. Success!

The learning in this scenario is twofold: first, even when under a time constraint, take time to do some problem solving and gather team member's thoughts on which solution should be implemented. The second lesson is that sometimes you need to let others fail so that they will learn. The caveat, of course, is that you minimize the risks incurred when that failure happens. We learn more from our failures more than our successes, so if the conditions are safe, allow the failure – and don't rub it in anyone's face!

Reflections

1. How do you feel about failure?
2. How can you embrace failure even more in your life?
3. What process will you use to reflect on failures and what you've learned from them?

Lesson #42: Good Enough Is Perfect

We only had 15 minutes left to access the President's secret bunker to disarm a nuclear bomb that would begin World War III. This was a close one – we didn't know how many more challenges we had to face before gaining access to the room that would allow us to turn off the ignition sequence. We found a bunch of scrabble pieces and believed that if we put them on a scrabble board near the door in the right words, we would uncover the five digits needed to open the door and gain access to the controls.

We had approximately 30 tiles that we needed to create words on the board. After only using 18 tiles to form the majority of five words, we were able to figure out the code without completing the full puzzle. We entered the five digits into the keypad, and the door popped open! We are happy to report that we stopped a potentially catastrophic event from occurring while most people were going about their regular days, not realizing the challenge we had just faced. You're welcome!

So often in life, we put too much pressure on ourselves to make sure everything is perfectly finished when most times "good enough" will suffice. One of us will never forget when, many years ago, a college professor stated that there is a finished paper, and there is a perfect paper, and the two will never be the same thing.

How much pressure are you putting on yourself to make sure everything is "perfect" – from the dinner party you are throwing to the project you are completing at work? Of course, there are some high-risk situations in which mistakes cannot be made;

however, let's be honest, we're often trying to reach for perfection in situations that do not call for it and putting ourselves under undue stress.

Reflections

1. Where in your life right now are you trying to reach perfection when "good enough" would suffice?
2. How can you be okay with "good enough" more often?
3. How will you determine in the future when you are putting undue stress on yourself in an attempt to reach perfection?

Lesson #43: Choose Your Tools Wisely

It was up to us to save the city. The evil villain's robot was recharging after having destroyed half the city, and we only had an hour to get in and foil his plan. We were inexperienced superheroes, but between us, we had various superpowers at our disposal. By switching between different items, we could use a different superpower: electromagnetism, super sight, super strength, etc. Our task was difficult, but, hey, it's the job of a superhero, right?

Sometimes in life, we have to make do with the tools we are given. In the case above, it was awesome to be able to switch our tools for the exact item we needed when we needed it. However, we don't always have that luxury in the real world. Our tools take more than just snapping in a module, disk, or attachment. Like tools, our knowledge, skills, and abilities don't work without effort and development, and if we haven't used them in a while, they won't be ready to go at a moment's notice. If we take the time to exercise our tools and take them out of the toolbag to keep them sharp, we can have a variety of useful things ready in a pinch.

Our times in escape rooms have also shown us that the right tool for a job may not always be apparent. We often find a tool, and suddenly, we can't see anything but the need for that tool. Like the saying, "If all you have is a hammer, everything looks like a nail." In reality, we are seldom limited to only the apparent tools or obvious way to use those tools. We've found magnets and looked for metal items to "grab," but it turns out that the magnet was a key to be placed on a wooden shelf. Or found a rod, thinking it needs to be put into a receptacle, but found a circular code around the base. And many times, we've found a tool that we will need in a later puzzle, but we lose a great deal of time trying to use it immediately.

In life, we have the option to choose our tools beforehand. There are a variety of different assessments available that can indicate a person's strengths and weaknesses. For example, Insights Discovery® is a tool that identifies personality leanings in your thoughts and behavior to thinking/feeling, introversion/extraversion, and sensing/intuition. By being aware of your tendencies, you can identify where you can contribute more, or how you can better integrate into the overall team performance.

Reflections

1. What tools do you have in your toolbox? When was the last time you used them?
2. Do you favor a specific ability? Is there a particular time when you've used that ability, but having different tools would have worked better?
3. Have you ever worked through a problem using a specific solution, and then later saw someone work through the same problem much easier using a different solution? How can you incorporate that into your toolbox?

Lesson #44: Make Time To Escape Reality

The average individual has a good amount of stress in their lives in this modern-day world. We all know how important it is to take a break from the daily grind to allow our bodies and minds to recuperate; however, not all of us understand the seriousness of just how important that break is. When you don't give your brain or body a break in a healthy way, the stress hormones build up in your system and wreak all kinds of havoc, eventually (or not so eventually) leading to sickness, disease, and even premature death.

We've used our escape room adventures as a great way to break free of the daily grind, giving our minds and bodies a special treat before heading back to the reality of daily life. Where else can you move your body and challenge your mind in a fun way while embarking on such adventures as saving humanity from a zombie virus or nuclear bomb, escaping prison, pillaging for treasure, or solving an infamous crime?

What are you currently doing to make sure your body and mind are ready and able to tackle life's issues that inevitably arise?

Reflections

1. How are you currently making time for your body and mind to recuperate from the daily stress of life?
2. How can you improve upon what you are currently doing?
3. Plan for breaks in your schedule over the next three months to ensure you are making recovering from the daily grind a priority.

Lesson #45: You Must Collaborate

A patient had escaped the asylum, which put the entire facility into lockdown. The doctors were trapped in their office, and the remaining patients were sealed in a padded room. The doctors could see the patients, and the patients could hear the doctors, but not vice versa. On top of that, the patients had medical restraint mitts (cuffing their hands together with a lock and covering their fingers). There was no way around it; we would have to work together to get out.

Many escape rooms add a challenging element where they divide the groups into teams that are physically separated. To progress, the teams have to figure out how to share information that is only available to one team but needed by the other team. This requires both sharing information and communicating it well.

In the case above, it was particularly difficult because we had ten people in the room together (five doctors and five patients). Communication is hard enough between two people. Add in everyone talking and sharing ideas, and it becomes very taxing and stressful. Once we were reunited, the patients couldn't remove the restraints without the help of one of the doctors, which added another stressor to one group that was mostly unfelt by the other group. It was hard to leave some people restrained while trying to find a way out. This perception of ignoring the needs of a person (i.e., "Hey, let me out first!") can interfere with communication and cause anxiety in the "trapped" person.

Few things can get accomplished without collaboration. When collaborating, it is important not only to expect others to provide information and help you but also for you to share information and help in a way that can be used by the receiver. This requires a great deal of patience and understanding since your success can be outside of your control. Also, it is important to be understanding in how information is provided to you. It is not always clear to the sender what the value of the information can be to you. They might be providing information in the hope that you will understand it even when they don't.

Reflections

1. When working in teams, do you get easily frustrated? What do you expect other team members to provide to you? Do you provide the same back to them?
2. How do you change the way you provide information and instructions based upon the recipient? How do you adjust your message?
3. When receiving information and instructions, do you expect the sender to explain everything, or do you make an effort to work it out yourself?

Lesson #46: You Always Have A Choice

We were waiting for our turn to get locked into yet another abandoned asylum. We were excited because this location spent a lot of time to create a Hollywood set-like feel to the rooms, immersing adventurers in the experience. Another group had gone into the room only 20 minutes before we arrived, so we knew we would be waiting for a while. We heard a few screams, and then the group quickly exited the room and left the building. We found out later that the room was too scary for some in the group, and they decided not to go through the entire experience.

We enjoyed the room and escaped with a little time to spare. Due to the immersion quality of the room, however, we could see how some individuals could get scared. The group that chose not to complete the room reminded us that we always have a choice in how we handle the situations in our lives.

Whether we are not happy at work, in a relationship that is not fulfilling, or have an experience we don't want to go through, we have a choice in how we respond. We can leave that job and find a new one that fulfills us, even if it means adjusting our lifestyle, or we can work on our perspective of how we view the job. We can choose to stay in a relationship and work on our perspective of how it fulfills us, or we can choose to leave the relationship. We can choose how we respond to and perceive the unpleasant experience we are going through.

Reflections

1. Examine the areas of your life in which you currently do not believe you have a choice and identify how it is a choice that you are making.
2. How can you improve your perspective to see that everything is a choice?
3. How does the idea that you always have a choice change your perspective on areas where you feel stuck?

Lesson #47: Increase Your Comfort Zone

Since we have completed hundreds of escape rooms, we love it when we can find those experiences that are a bit different than the rest. For this adventure, we found ourselves handcuffed, hooded, and led into a noisy room. Our captor made us each get into a coffin and shut the lid. Unfortunately, our team of investigators had gotten too close to catching the elusive Moriarity, and he had us buried alive. Yikes! We knew ahead of time that we were required to complete the mission while locked in a box, but it had only become a reality the moment we were actually locked in. One of our team members had to take a moment to breathe through a claustrophobic feeling, but after a couple of minutes, they were back in the game and ready to face the challenge.

We worked together through a small hole drilled between our coffins, finding out at what location we were buried, and calling the authorities to rescue us. Phew – 43 minutes in a box can be exhilarating and exhausting! What was important about this experience is that it took us out of our comfort zones.

The following graphic depicts the different "zones" in which we can find ourselves. The innermost circle represents our comfort zone (the "green" zone). This zone is where we feel safe and competent. We know what we're doing, and we have complete control over things. The center circle represents our stretch zone (the "yellow" zone). This zone is where we are a bit uncomfortable as we don't have complete control, and we're learning and growing (thus expanding our comfort zone). The outer circle represents the panic zone (the "red" zone). This zone is where we feel completely out-of-control, we are anxious, and things are going way too fast for us.

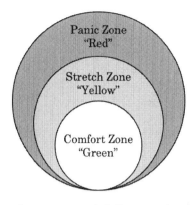

Unfortunately, according to Karl Albrecht in his book, *Practical Intelligence*, most people stick within their comfort zone, meaning most individuals develop themselves only as much as necessary to cope in their current environment. Only about 20% of folks continue learning and growing throughout their lives. Yikes! When we don't take the time to develop ourselves further, this leads to a narrowing of both the range and the depth of our thinking processes.

To develop ourselves, we need to spend the majority of our time in the stretch zone, pushing ourselves each day to develop further. Reflective journaling, reading a book, taking a course, and listening to a podcast are a few ways one can further develop themselves (if they're educational, of course!). It's okay to retreat to our comfort zone occasionally for a breather; however, let's not live there!

Reflections

1. How are you living in your stretch zone?
2. Are you ensuring that you're pushing yourself each day to develop yourself further?
3. How can you live in your stretch zone more?

Lesson #48: Sh*t Happens

Escape rooms have gone through an evolution since the first ones opened. PanIQ had a great explanation on their website of the different generations of the rooms. From the first generation (basic locks, very low technology) to the third generation rooms (no or very few traditional locks, very high technology). As the market works to improve the experience and "wow factor," it is inevitable that when playing, you'll run into things going wrong, which is why it's important to remember that sh*t happens!

We were in a newly opened room, working our way through a tomb. Because of some technical issues, the game master was physically in the room with us, and at one point, in the beginning, we had to restart the room. This was a lesson in sh*t happens. When we started having technology problems, the game master "stopped the clock" and asked us to feel free to keep working while he stepped out to work an electronic glitch. What could have been a very frustrating experience for both the game master and us, turned out to be very low stress. We ended up having a lot of fun interacting face-to-face with the game master. This was our first game at that location; we played all six of their rooms in a row (with dinner between rooms four and five). By the end, we knew the names of everyone working there that day, we traded experiences, and they rooted for us in each room.

In all aspects of our lives, we can experience setbacks, mistakes, or frustrations. How those experiences shape our feelings and behaviors, though, is up to us. By taking things in stride, minding our emotions, and acknowledging problems without annoyance, we can make the best of many situations, and even improve the outcome for everyone.

As teammates in escape rooms, we find that we can identify when one of us is getting frustrated, and most of the time, simply pointing out the signs is enough to reset and bring us "back down." Escape rooms, and life in general, are about having fun, good experiences, and self-improvement. And, remember, sh*t happens!

Reflections

1. Can you recognize when you are getting frustrated? Are you able to work through it?
2. Do you have someone who can help you identify when you are reacting to things going wrong? Do you have a plan in place to change your perception?
3. Compare times you've had a bad experience and a good experience when things were going wrong. What was different about you in those cases?

Lesson #49: Take Small Bites

It is always impressive when a complex problem can be explained in a simple way (much more impressive than a simple problem being explained in a complex way). Similar to explaining a complex problem, understanding a complex problem boils down to breaking it into smaller, easier to understand pieces. You've heard of this process when you hear the phrases "simplify," "divide and conquer," or "keep it simple." You've probably even done this process if you've tried to solve a jigsaw puzzle. Did you start with the center or the edges? Many people start with the edges because it means you have one piece of information right from the start. In standardized testing, we are told if you can eliminate two of four answers, then you have a higher probability of getting it right (or at least you have a 50% chance). When faced with a puzzle, start with the pieces or aspects that let you narrow down some of the complexity.

When you can, try to arrange your information in a way that helps to solve pieces of the puzzle. We frequently have to complete pictures, diagrams, or charts. By arranging pieces into groups (e.g., all pieces with red wires in one pile, or all the diamonds with red on the right), you can then look for a specific piece of information (e.g., I need a piece with a red wire on it or a diamond that matches red on the left). In this way, very complex problems can become easier and quicker to solve.

This approach can also be used in many other situations. For example, improving the performance of a team can start by improving the performance of a few members, or even just one member. In other cases, start with the problems you can fix now, and any additional problems can be addressed when you get to them. Many problems become less of an issue when other seemingly unrelated matters become resolved.

Moreover, when completing projects, we tend to want to use the same tool, or person, throughout. By breaking a problem into its parts, it becomes easier to see options for other tools or using other people's strengths. No one has built a skyscraper by themselves.

Reflections

1. When faced with a complex problem or project, how do you organize it?
2. What are some ways you can break it down to even smaller bites to address one at a time?
3. What are some other creative ways you can tackle big problems or projects?

Lesson #50: Everything Is Negotiable

In yet another undisclosed location in Europe, we escaped from a post-apocalyptic vault and saved humanity (you're welcome – again!). Even though the booking software for the company said that there was a minimum of three people needed for the room, we still signed up for it, hoping they'd let us play with two people when we got there. Once we arrived, the game master shared quite a long monologue (that got emotional at times) about how she wanted us to have a good experience; how she went through it with just two people and it was a horrible experience; and while she would leave it up to us if we wanted to continue, she thought we shouldn't.

Of course, we played the room and had a blast! We escaped the vault, overthrew the evil robots, shot our way out of the robot's military zone, and crawled through the sewers (which thankfully did not smell like sewers) to get back up to the Earth's surface. The only frustrating moments we had were when we interacted with the game master who was not paying attention to our progress as she should have been and kept giving clues to things we had already solved.

We had quite a bit of learning from this experience, and we hope the game master learned a little something as well. The primary learning point; everything is negotiable. We were able to convince the game master that two individuals can have completely different experiences of the same situation. Don't let a "no" deter you – build rapport with the person attempting to dissuade you, and if you want to go after something – find a way to do it!

Reflections

1. Reflect on a recent time you had to negotiate with someone about something you wanted to do. How did it go?
2. What are some ways you can work on your negotiation skills to improve them?
3. What are you going to do differently in your next negotiation?

Pro Tip #5: Pigpen Cipher

Another interesting cryptogram that we see frequently is called the pigpen cipher. It is composed of a key, in the form of a grid or shape with letters and dots, and a code composed of figures that represent the position in the grid or shape and whether there is a dot or not. With the key, you can translate the code into unique characters.

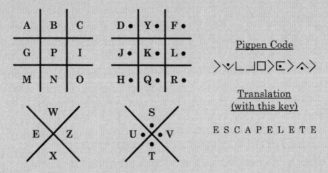

Pigpen Code

Translation (with this key)

ESCAPELETE

We have even run into the templar variation in a historically researched escape room (good job on the part of the game designer!), although this variation only uses 25 characters. These codes can be disguised into cells in a table, portions of windows, written text, or on specific items.

Templar Code

Translation (with this key)

MALTESE CROSS

Lesson #51: Digging In The Toilet

We were stranded out in the woods with no cell reception. Our car had crashed into a tree, and we were hiking to a nearby ranger station to get help. It was getting dark as we approached the log cabin, and strange sounds were coming from the woods all around us. We quickly ran into the cabin and locked the door, finding it empty - the ranger was nowhere to be seen. We had to figure out how to get the radio working and get help. As we searched the cabin, we noticed a key in the water of the outhouse-style toilet. "Not it!" one partner immediately exclaimed. Dang – that left the other to go fishing. There are a surprising number of important things in toilets in escape rooms.

We all have tasks in life that are disagreeable. Nevertheless, sometimes we have to get through those unpleasant tasks to reach our end goal. Many times, like in escape rooms, putting off the inevitable only sets us back.

One tactic is to be mentally prepared to dive right in. This can work reasonably well and does have the advantage of saving time. It likewise helps to have fun with it. From creating a game or process to handle the tasks, it can also destigmatize negative mental perceptions of the task itself.

While it is good to be prepared to dive right in, it is also equally important to take a moment to see if there is an alternative solution. In the case of the toilet, one of us had already reached in and grabbed the key before the other noticed a small net that could have prevented the other one from having to put a hand in the oily water.

The world is full of unpleasant tasks that need to get completed. From going to the gym, to completing paperwork or reports, to finally cleaning out the garage, we can make unpleasant tasks less unpleasant by jumping right in, making a game of it, or changing our mindset about the task itself.

Reflections

1. Is there a task you've been putting off? How can you change your perception of the task to help you get it done?
2. How does delaying an unpleasant task weigh on your mind? How does it affect you even when you're not doing it?
3. How can you make a game out of a boring or mundane task you currently have to do?

Lesson #52: Face Your Fears

The back of the cabinet opened up into a murky corridor. We had no light, and the only way forward was through the dark. In the swirling smoke that kept pouring in through vents in the walls, it was hard to see that the far door had a sliding peephole to look into the dimly lit room and see the immobile body under the white sheet. Wait - did the body move? Our plan to talk with the restless spirit of a murder victim who had died in this abandoned house was getting a little scary.

Whether it's finding yourself locked in a coffin, getting hooded and handcuffed, climbing through narrow crawl spaces, or just sticking your arm into some unknown crevice, escape rooms are a great way to challenge your fears. One way or another, it will be over in approximately an hour! You don't have to find a scary or horror-themed escape room to challenge your fears, but they certainly help you face and overcome them if you're willing.

Many of us like to feel in control of our daily lives. We may stay in an unfulfilling job, keep quiet when we know the answer, or do the same things over and over because we can guarantee the same results. Not facing our fears of what might happen if we change things around may lead to a mundane and growth-averse life. Like building muscles and endurance, our personal development needs stressors, resistance, and effort. Without those things, we can't build ourselves up.

We need to challenge our limits and emotions to build knowledge, skill, and talent "muscle." From speaking out when we're not comfortable, to holding back and giving someone else a try, facing our fears takes effort.

Reflections

1. What are you afraid of doing (for example, is it public speaking)? How can you challenge that fear in small doses?
2. What opportunities are you or could you be missing by not stepping up? How can you volunteer for additional new experiences?
3. What is at the heart of your fear? How can you overcome this?

Lesson #53: Be Prepared For Anything

We started our adventure by digging through a pile of Triceratops poop – yep, you read that right. We had to diagnose what was making her sick and prepare a shot with the right combination of medicine to help her. Shortly after that, we found out that several velociraptors had escaped their cage, so we needed to evacuate the lab for our safety while they were captured.

We were able to make it to the outer gate and entered the code in the keypad to initiate our escape. We were excited to make it out before getting eaten, but nothing happened. The gate didn't open. We soon found out why – a huge Tyrannosaurus Rex's head came over the gate! Its head was as big as a VW Bug, with teeth as large as our heads. Luckily, as it was dipping down over the gate to take a bite of us, a small passageway opened up next to the gate, and we were able to crawl to our safety.

In escape rooms, one doesn't always know what they're walking into or, in the case of most U.S. escape rooms, with whom one is walking into it. These are escape rooms – anything can happen! Such as in life – we can make plans, but we must be prepared for anything. Sometimes the surprises we face can be great opportunities; other times, they may be the changes in our lives that we do not desire. Regardless, the more flexible and adaptable we are, the more we will be able to face whatever comes our way.

Reflections

1. How flexible and adaptable are you?
2. How can you improve your ability to handle it when something unexpected occurs?
3. How can you prepare yourself for anything that could occur in the future?

Lesson #54: Remain Calm Under Pressure

We found ourselves trapped in the engine room of an abandoned ship. We only had 60 minutes to liberate ourselves before the ship sunk beneath the waves, and we became shark bait. We were able to work our way past the engine room through the captain's quarters, and after crawling through a very small tunnel, we found ourselves close to freedom. The escape hatch was within reach. Unfortunately, it was locked (of course!).

We examined the room, flipping various switches on the control panel to see if we could trip the door. One of us did something to set off a piercing alarm, and water started pouring into the room. It looked like the ship was going to sink faster than we thought. We were standing on top of a grate, and just as soon as one of us mentioned that the water wouldn't rise above the grate, it did – and it kept coming. We had to climb up on the counters in the room to keep from getting our shoes and pants wet.

At this point in the experience, stress took over (at least for one of us). With the blaring alarm, the rising water, and the clock counting down, it became almost impossible to think straight. The teammate who was not reacting to the imposed stress began working on getting the alarm to turn off by focusing on the only puzzle that could be reached without getting off the counter. The other partner retreated into the captain's quarters to take a breather as we are well aware that we cannot effectively solve problems when under acute stress. Thankfully, the alarms were silenced, the short break helped, and while we had to wade our way through the water, we were able to unlock the escape hatch and free ourselves from the ship before it sunk below the surface.

Too often in life, we find ourselves under pressure and neglect to manage our emotional response before trying to forge ahead. Unfortunately, the stress response, if not handled as it arises, leads to poor decisions and an inability to effectively problem solve.

Reflections

1. Are you aware of when you are under pressure and having a stress response? How do you know you are aware?
2. What strategies do you use to address your stress response and ultimately remain calm under pressure?
3. How can you improve addressing your stress response for future situations?

Lesson #55: It's Not About You

As humans, this is a lesson we all must learn – "it is not about me." Our brains are wired to be concerned primarily with the self as a 10,000-year-old survival mechanism. In our modern era, where getting eaten by a saber tooth tiger is not a major concern, we have to overcome our brain's inclination towards being so self-focused.

Escape rooms are a great way to retrain yourself to focus on the outcomes (escaping) rather than your performance (how many puzzles I solved by myself). We have been in escape rooms with various groups of individuals, and at times, have found ourselves with someone who, after our team enjoys a successful escape, seeks reassurance because they did not feel like they contributed to the team enough. Often, reminding the individual of the various roles they played in facing the challenges doesn't seem to provide the assurance they were seeking.

Instead, through our escape room experiences, we have learned not to tie our individual performance into the outcome. Sometimes we have been "killing it" and doing very well facing the challenges and still did not escape the room. Other times, we got very lucky, not performing well at all, and successfully escaped the room. Escape room experiences teach us to set our egos aside and participate with the team in the best way we can – the team's success is our success.

Reflections

1. Reflect on the last time you were more focused on your performance rather than the outcome you were seeking. How was that experience for you?
2. How can you change your perspective to be less focused on you and your performance?
3. How can you prepare for your next experience to ensure you make it less about you?

Lesson #56: Be Careful With Wishful Thinking

A framed definition we saw on the walls at *Can You Escape? Malta* was: "Illusory Correlation: seeing the connection between two disconnected items. Informally referred to as 'wishful thinking.' Tends to happen when participants run out of ideas." Wishful thinking can happen in many ways in an escape room, from thinking you have more time, or a puzzle will take less time, to refusing to ask for clues because you are sure you can figure it out. In many instances, this can lead to wasting effort going down rabbit holes or working hunches that don't pan out. In the worst cases, we've seen people try to take apart furniture or break open locks.

In our professional and personal lives, wishful thinking can happen when we try to force cause-and-effect associations, underestimate the time and effort needed for a task or project, or assume that relationships can be sustained without contributions and concessions on both sides. While ambitious plans and enthusiastic efforts are worthwhile, realistic expectations are reasonable and can inform more practical steps to getting to your lofty goals. You can get there by doing it in smaller increments or with help.

Additionally, recognizing incontrovertible boundaries and constraints (e.g., gravity and reduced flexibility as we age) is not giving up. Admitting boundaries and weaknesses are just as necessary as acknowledging strengths and successes. They are not good or bad in and of themselves. They are inputs to your plans and goals and can be addressed and overcome with determination and help. As Albert Einstein said, "The definition of insanity is doing the same thing over and over again, but expecting different results." Recognize those things you can affect, and those you can't and focus on those you can without wasting time on "wishful thinking."

Reflections

1. How long do you work on an issue or relationship before seeking help? How can you learn to ask for help earlier?
2. Are you aware of your boundaries and weaknesses? How do you acknowledge them without giving up?
3. Have you ever had a belief or assumption that turned out to be false? What did you learn from the realization?

Lesson #57: Create Silence

An outline of the body was on the floor. It appears that in the person's dying moments, they pointed to a clue to locate the perpetrator of their demise. Our team of highly skilled investigators had been brought in to identify the murderer and uncover their motive. It appeared to be a perfect crime – until we were able to decipher the first clue, which led to the next, and then another, and so on.

At one point in the investigation, we reached a very difficult piece of evidence to decipher. Interestingly, at the same time, what was previously background music in the room, started becoming quite loud. It was almost impossible to think. Our team had to take a moment to close our eyes, take some deep breathes, and do our best to block out the noise while working through the puzzle. Thankfully, we were able to push through, solve the challenge, and the music faded away to background music once again. We successfully identified the murderer and their motive before he trapped us in the room forever.

How often in life are we faced with excessive noise in our environments (literally and figuratively)? Studies have shown that excessive noise around us can release a hormone into the brain that hinders both planning and reasoning. When there is too much going on in our heads, or we're surrounded with too much noise (music, background conversations, and so on), we cannot think clearly enough to face whatever challenge we need to overcome. The strategy to resolve this issue is to remove ourselves from the noise and find a way to create silence, if only for a few minutes. For noise within your mind, meditation works very well to help train you to seek a moment of silence. For noise outside your brain, you can remove yourself from the area, or if you can't, take a moment to go within and practice some deep breathing.

Reflections

1. How much noise (internal or external) is in your life?
2. How are you currently creating silence when needed?
3. What are some new strategies you could implement to help create silence more effectively in the future?

Lesson #58: Enjoy The Process

We found ourselves on another pirate ship. This time we were locked in separate cells in the brig and had the mission of freeing ourselves from the cells, going through the captain's quarters to find a map revealing the location of hidden treasure, and then finding a way off the ship. We felt like we were really on a pirate ship because of the set-like quality of the room. We had to take a moment to enjoy the scenery and take in every detail that the game designer put into our immersive experience.

By paying close attention to the immersive quality of the room, we were able to locate a few clues that we may not have noticed when one gets the typical tunnel vision while zeroing in on completing a challenging task. We accomplished our mission, victoriously escaping the ship with map in hand. Our game master celebrated with us after the escape and said, "it's nice to see players appreciate the room."

Too often in life, we are focused on the destination and not appreciating the journey it takes to get there. We run into this a lot in the world of escape rooms. People want to solve the puzzles as fast as possible so they can get on the "leader board," which ranks the teams that get out of the room the fastest. When the game master delivers the pre-brief for each room, they usually share the requirements to get on the leader board. We respond that we want to get out with two minutes to spare, not to clear the room in 20 minutes. We are paying good money for a quality experience, so why would we want to cut it short?

Think about how this applies to your goals in life. You set a goal for yourself (professional or personal) and then do what you can to achieve it in the fastest way possible. What about really enjoying the process of who you become while going after that goal?

Reflections

1. In what areas of your life do you need to take time to enjoy the journey?
2. In your current goals, how can you change your focus on the process of who you become in accomplishing them?
3. For future goals, how can you ensure that you are focused on the process of achieving them just as much as the actual achievement of them?

Lesson #59: Try New Things

It was our daughter's 21st birthday. For this special milestone birthday, she wanted to visit the Wizarding World of Harry Potter at Universal Studios in Orlando. We made it through the various sites we wanted to see during the trip pretty quickly, so we looked around for a few other fun things to do – Orlando has many of those after all.

Our daughter found a location near to our hotel that had escape rooms, something we had never heard of before. She requested that we try one out, and when we found out that it involved being locked in a room for an hour, solving a series of puzzles to get out, we were reluctant to try the new experience. For whatever reason (which we can't recall after so much fun over the years), we didn't find the idea appealing – how could this experience be fun?

The very next day, we showed up at our appointed time and were led into a tomb we had been tasked with raiding. This experience wasn't at all like what we had created in our minds. It looked like a cave, and there were no obvious "puzzles" around that we had to solve. Soon, we were on the hunt to figure out how to accomplish our mission and find the lost jewel. After manipulating a few items in the cave, we pulled a lever, and the wall moved! We found another room with even more clues to solve. Passing over the threshold into a deeper part of the cave is the moment we became hooked! It also helped that our game master was cheering for us and nudged us as we got stuck at various times throughout the experience. We went back the next day and did another three rooms.

At the time we are publishing this book, we have done hundreds of rooms in nine countries and fifteen states. Needless to say that by pushing out of our comfort zone and trying something new, we have uncovered an addiction that has led to many fun times together, sometimes with friends and loved ones, and a way to combine our passion for learning with fun.

How often do you find yourself saying "yes" to new experiences? As long as it is a safe and healthy experience, why not try it? The more novel experiences we provide our brains, the more neural pathways we build, and the younger we can keep our brains.

Reflections

1. How often are you engaging in new experiences?
2. What benefits do new experiences bring you?
3. How can you engage in even more novel experiences in your life (personally and professionally)?

Lesson #60: It's Okay To Be A Little Crazy!

We've thoroughly enjoyed our escape room journey and hope that our enjoyment of these experiences continues into our twilight years. When we first started talking about our passion with others, we weren't quite sure how we felt about people's incredulous looks as some had never heard of escape rooms and couldn't believe how enthusiastic we were about them. Now we enjoy those looks, and more and more people are relating to us as escape rooms have become more of a mainstream concept.

We don't mind being a little crazy about escape rooms – well, let's be honest – A LOT crazy about escape rooms. We've turned this into a book, blog, speech, workshop, online course, and Christina uses these examples of learning in all of her speeches and workshops. Here's the thing, folks - people may think you're crazy to follow your dream (and that's okay!). If you are truly passionate about something (that is legal, ethical, and all that other important stuff), then go for it. Don't hide talking about it from others because you're worried about what they will think.

Reflections

1. What are you totally crazy about?
2. Are you sharing your passion with others?
3. What can you do to share your passion even more? (write a book, launch a podcast, write a blog, etc.).

Final Thoughts

The only person you are destined to become is the person you decide to be.

—Ralph Waldo Emerson

In our research for this book, we were dismayed to find out that most people stick to what they know. They develop themselves only as much as necessary to cope in their current environment. As we mentioned in *Lesson #47: Increase Your Comfort Zone*, according to Karl Albrecht, only about 20% of folks continue learning and growing throughout their lives. When we don't take time to develop ourselves further, we greatly narrow both the range and the depth of our thinking processes. Who wants only to exist? Let's aim for a thriving life!

A mind that faces challenges is a mind that grows. This is why we thought escape rooms would be the perfect medium for learning about how to be successful in life. While they are fun, they can also provide us with invaluable learning opportunities that we can apply to our personal and professional lives.

We hope you've enjoyed our escape experiences and what we've learned from them as much as we have. Thank you for going on this journey with us.

Acknowledgments

We want to thank *Escape Room Live Georgetown* both for their great rooms and experiences, as well as allowing us to do a photo shoot at their location. We always have a great time in their rooms, and the set-like quality is amazing!

We want to thank *Can You Escape? Malta,* for taking the time to talk with us and rearrange the order of our booked rooms; so we could see the evolution of your game design. In addition to being super supportive while we went through your great rooms, we also liked all of the definitions you had on your walls that you graciously provided us with to reference in this book.

We also want to thank the Escape Room Enthusiasts Facebook page for the camaraderie and great suggestions on places to try. It's wonderful knowing others out there share our passions!

And, to all the escape room owners and game masters out there who make escaping so fantastic, our thanks and a request to keep the amazing experiences coming!

Last, but certainly not least, we want to thank the fellow escapeletes that have helped us both experience the stories within this book as well as ensure that we told them in the most effective way possible.

About the Authors

Christina M. Eanes

Through more than fifteen years of public service with a California police department and the Federal Bureau of Investigation (FBI), Christina worked on an array of programs, including the FBI's Violent Criminal Apprehension Program (ViCAP) and the FBI's Leadership Development Program, where she helped train thousands of leaders.

After advancing to a senior manager position within the FBI before turning forty, Christina decided to open her own business to help people transform their personal and professional lives. Check out her websites at ChristinaEanes.com, QuitBleepingAround.com, and SecretToSuperProductivity.com.

Jeffrey W. Eanes

With 27 years of public service, Jeffrey followed five years of civilian emergency medical response experience by going on active duty in 1995 as a combat medic assigned to the 82nd Airborne Division in the U.S. Army. Upon completing his Masters of Public Administration after his military service, Jeffrey made his way through several civilian positions within the Department of Defense, spending the majority of his time in the Office of the Secretary of Defense, where he works on organization, management, and statutory issues.

Chris and Jeff live in the Alexandria, Virginia, area, enjoying several escapecations a year to keep the learning alive for both themselves and you!

Additional Resources

Escapeletes.com

This website chronicles Chris and Jeff's learning as they tackle escape rooms around the world. Also, check out recommended escape room locations and the latest number of escape rooms the team has completed.

QuitBleepingAround.com

What to accomplish more in your life? This website contains several resources to help you get out of your own way in your achievement efforts. This includes Christina's first book, *Quit Bleeping Around: 77 Secrets to Superachieving*, and the Quit Bleeping Around podcast, currently listened to in more than 77 countries.

TheSecretToSuperProductivity.com

Desire to be more productive? This website features Christina's second book, *The Secret to Super Productivity: Because Time is Not Your Most Limiting Resource*. Check it out to see how you can create more hours in your week.

ChristinaEanes.com

This website contains a list of programs Christina and her team of instructors and coaches offer to clients in the leadership and professional development areas. When doing team building activities, Christina will often bring an "escape box" to offer clients the opportunity to have fun "escaping" while learning to work more closely together.

References

Albrecht, Karl. *Practical Intelligence: The Art and Science of Common Sense*, 2007.

Branson, Richard. *QuoteFancy*. https://quotefancy.com/quote/899315/Richard-Branson-Take-a-chance-it-s-the-best-way-to-test-yourself-have-fund-and-push.

Cambridge Brain Sciences. "Active Video Games Power Up Cognition." 2019. Retrieved from https://www.cambridgebrainsciences.com/more/articles/active-video-games-boost-cognition.

Definitions. [Posters] Exhibited at Can You Escape? Malta, July 2019.

Donnelly, Laura. "Brain training games boost memory and may reduce the risk of dementia, research suggests." *The Telegraph*, July 2017. https://www.telegraph.co.uk/science/2017/07/02/brain-training-games-boost-memory-may-reduce-risk-dementia-research/.

Emerson, Ralph Waldo. *PassItOn*. https://www.passiton.com/inspirational-quotes/6638-the-only-person-you-are-destined-to-become-is.

Gaffney, Maureen. *Flourishing*, 2011.

Gladwell, Malcolm. *Outliers: The Story of Success*, 2008.

Insights Discovery. https://www.insights.com/us/what-we-do/our-story/.

PanIQ. "Escape Room Generations." December 2019. https://paniqescaperoom.com/blog/escape-room-generations/.

Pink, Dan. "The puzzle of motivation." *TEDGlobal 2009*, July 2009. Retrieved from https://www.ted.com/talks/dan_pink_the_puzzle_of_motivation.

Restak, Richard M.D. *The Naked Brain: How the Emerging Neurosociety is Changing How We Live, Work, and Love*, 2006.

Spira, Lisa. *5 Year US Escape Room Industry Report*, August 2019. Room Escape Artist. https://roomescapeartist.com/.

Stanmore, Emma, et al. "The effect of active video games on cognitive functioning in clinical and non-clinical populations: A meta-analysis of a randomized controlled trial." Neuroscience & Biobehavioral Reviews, July 2017. https://www.sciencedirect.com/science/article/pii/S014976341730129X#ack0005.

United States Census Bureau. https://www.census.gov/.

Van Hoenselaar, Mike. *Escape Rooms in the World: Insights, trends, and challenges of one of the biggest growths in the leisure industry!* Escape Room Stats Identity Games 2019_Updated. info@escaperoomsnederland.nl. escaperoomsnederland.nl.

Von Moltke, Helmuth. *Wikiquote.*
https://en.wikiquote.org/wiki/Helmuth_von_M
oltke_the_Elder.

Wikipedia. *Braille, Duck Test, Escape Room, Game,
Morse Code, PigPen Cipher.*
https://www.wikipedia.org/.

Made in the USA
Middletown, DE
21 February 2020